BUILDING
YOUR
CHILD'S
FAITH

OTHER BOOKS BY ALICE CHAPIN

Let The Living Bible Help You
Bible Promises for Supernatural Living
400 Ways to Say "I Love You"
Bright Ideas for Creative Parents
Reaching Back

Building Your Child's Faith

ALICE CHAPIN

THOMAS NELSON PUBLISHERS
Nashville

Published in Nashville, Tennessee, by Thomas Nelson,
Inc., and distributed in Canada by Lawson Falle, Ltd.,
Cambridge, Ontario.

Printed in the United States of America.

Scripture quotations are from the NEW KINGS JAMES
VERSION of the Bible. Copyright © 1979, 1980, 1982,
Thomas Nelson, Inc., Publishers.

Library of Congress Cataloging-in-Publication Data

Chapin, Alice Zillman.
    Building your child's faith / Alice Chapin.
      p.   cm.
    ISBN 0-8407-3134-5
    1. Christian education—Home training. 2. Christian
education of children. 3. Children—Religious life. I. Title.
BV1590.C49   1990
248.8'45—dc20   90–32644
                                          CIP

Printed in the United States of America
2 3 4 5 6 7 — 95 94 93 92 91 90

To Beth Wilson, my first grandchild.
I love you, Beth.

CONTENTS

CHAPTER 1

Kids Need God Too!

My son, if you receive my words,
So that you incline your ear to wisdom, . . .
Then you will understand righteousness
  and justice,
Equity and every good path.

When wisdom enters your heart,
And knowledge is pleasant to your soul,
Discretion will preserve you;
Understanding will keep you,
To deliver you from the way of evil.

> —The words of a loving father
> to his son (Prov. 2:1-12)

I want to join you moms and dads in one of the most rewarding and exciting journeys of life—passing on the faith to your children and becoming spiritual parents and grandparents. Many of you already agree that responsibility for teaching children about God is not transferable and that it belongs squarely with parents by divine decree. But today's busy mothers and fathers tell me they often feel overwhelmed by the fact that they only have twenty years or fewer to fulfill this responsibility and that there is no second chance to get the job done. They often feel inadequate too. They worry when newspaper feature stories report that children are sometimes easily led into witchcraft or some other awful path and that parents sometimes must pay thousands of dollars to kidnap mixed-up young people back from cult groups. Many parents sense that a child who grows up with a strong biblical knowledge and with a faith that produces helpful resources in times of trouble is not so likely to be enticed by every new religious wind that blows past. But how does one accomplish this awesome task?

To help, I began collecting successful ideas from men and women in my seminars, "How to Share Your Faith with Your Children." I believe parents *can* succeed with or without a great knowledge of Scripture, a college or high school diploma, or a gift for eloquent speaking.

Who influenced your life to help make you what you are today?

Marla, age twenty, was brought up in a deeply religious home. She says, "One of my earliest and best memories is of Mother singing 'Rock of Ages' in the kitchen. I learned to pray by listening to Daddy during family devotions every Tuesday and Thursday evening. When kids called me 'Fatty' in the third grade, it meant a lot to think to myself, 'If God loves me like the Bible says, then I must be worth something.' I knew I must still be valuable in spite of being overweight. Once, when I didn't want to go to school because other kids made fun of me, Mom took me aside and first with a hug, then with a long and loving look straight into my eyes, reminded me to claim my heritage as a daughter of the King of kings. When she read Psalm 139 to me, it made me feel better."

One young mother says her small son refreshed her own faith: "My eyes were red, and our six-year-old, Danny, knew I had been crying because I missed my dad who had died at the age of forty-nine just three weeks before. Danny left his LEGOs on the floor where he had been playing. He came over to place his little hand on mine as I sat wiping my tears over a cup of Saturday morning coffee at the kitchen table. He missed his Grampy too, but I knew he wanted to comfort me. 'Don't cry, Mamma,' he said. 'Grampy's with Jesus. Bet he could push back the clouds with his hands and make a b-i-i-i-g-g opening to look down on us. Bet he's watching you blow your nose right now. Grampy's happy in heaven, Mamma. The Bible says so.' Suddenly it all became true again—the resurrection of the dead and the fact of heaven—as I heard my son attest gallantly to the beliefs we had shared with him."

Children can be taught to put their faith to work. Yet Bible illiteracy is real and growing. According to one Gallup poll, only about one-third of college students attend church regularly and only four in ten teens believe religion is increasing its influence in American lives. Other polls show that in the last twenty years, the percentage of adults who claim to have received no religious instruction has doubled. Two-thirds of young people in evangelical churches never read the Bible. Merton Strommen, director of the Search Institute in Minneapolis, cites one explanation for the lack of Bible reading. He found that 54 percent of children who attend church never hear their parents discuss the Bible, God, or any religious topic. Writer Philip Yancey adds that even those teens who do read the Bible meet major frustrations because they see it as a bewildering and boring thousand-page maze. Kids need our help finding their way around in the Bible.

Says one high school senior through tears, "I always thought rules were to make me miserable. I thought that I had the right to run my life. Now I have herpes and feel so alone. Finally, after studying the Bible with friends, I see that God loved us enough to give us a handbook for better living and Jesus to wipe out our sins. I never took God's view of sex very seriously until now. Now I believe that guidelines from both the Old and New Testaments were given because God loves us and wants the best for us. It's very touching to me that He would care so much, but how I wish I had discovered all this earlier!"

"I believe a child's spiritual condition is the controlling factor behind what he will become," says Zig Ziglar in his book *Raising Positive Kids in a Negative World.* A youngster's early training may well determine whether or not he can accept his lot in life contentedly. Indeed, it may determine his belief that there is a God to depend on. The most natural place to teach a child about God is at the parent's knee. Mom and Dad have the patience, love, and motivation to get the job done best.

The loving ultimatum to parents to accomplish this task is clear and it comes from God Himself:

You shall love the LORD your God with all your heart, with all your soul, and with all your might. And these words which I command you today shall be in your heart; you shall teach them diligently to your children, and shall talk of them when you sit in your house, when you walk by the way, when you lie down, and when you rise up (Deut. 6:5–7).

Moms and dads can deliver the doctrine a child needs at handy times in just the right-sized doses— holding parent-child conversations, rocking, doing dishes together, playing on the floor, smelling flowers, hiking, sitting around the dinner table, or getting ready for bed as well as during planned times. This teaching style can help to insure that later, as an adult, our children will not be confused. They will not struggle with the basics of the faith because they will have mastered them and found them workable long before the extra pressures of adult life close in.

Where is stability in life? Nearly one family in

five picks up and moves every year, twelve to fourteen times in a lifetime. With a 50 percent divorce rate in first marriages and 75 percent among second-timers in America, kids are often ripped apart from parents they love deeply. Since three-quarters of divorced people do remarry, curious and sometimes unloving or unwelcome new combinations of people end up living under one roof. Divorce has also left behind more than fourteen million single women who never do remarry and must support families and thousands of lonely after-school latchkey children. Even the definition of sin has changed, and some "experts" have declared sin non-existent. The difference between right and wrong seems blurred by talk of relative values. Unlike a few years ago, confused teenagers commonly see pregnant, single junior high and high school girls in campus corridors, and researchers tell us that by age twenty, three-fourths of young men and women in America are no longer virgins. Today's children often feel intimidated into wearing unfamiliar fashion fads like miniskirts and punk haircuts that come and go in a few months. To add to all this fluctuation, important people like parents and grandparents die. Teachers retire, friends move away, and friendly old buildings are bulldozed into a sad heap to make room for new structures. Our kids need security. They need to be able to count on at least one unchanging constant in life. When they know about Him, they can find this constancy in God.

On a plane to Florida, I chatted with an aerospace engineer whose college-age son had recently found his way into Bible studies with a group of Christian students on campus. This brilliant man confided, "I'm worried about Kim because I don't know whether he's gotten into something harmless and transitory or something dangerous or kooky or wonderful. I don't have enough spiritual know-how to determine that. Worse, Kim is asking me to read the Bible and follow Christ too. He says he has found peace he never had before. I don't even think religion is necessary. Look how far I've come without it! I earn more money than most people I know, own an elegant home in the best part of town with a built-in pool and tennis courts, belong to the most exclusive country club in the county, and have famous friends in Washington, D.C. Besides all that, I'm well respected and not a bad guy."

"Where do you go for help when you are sick or in trouble?" I asked.

"Well, last year I did have a bad heart attack. It scared the dickens out of me, but I depended on my wife, the wisdom of one of the top heart specialists in the country, and then on a private nurse." He paused a moment. "My wife died six months ago."

I continued, "Doctors are not infallible, nor do they live forever. Suppose yours had been killed in a car accident and the nurse had been kept home by sickness when you needed her. Or suppose you had been taken ill on the lonely Appalachian Trail, miles away from any human help. Who would you have depended on then?"

There was a long silence. "I guess I would have to depend on myself . . ." His voice trailed off.

"But you were very ill . . ." I reminded him.

He saw my point. This well educated and independent man had no further answer. He quickly saw the need for some higher person to care about him and comfort him when friends dropped away. Sadly, like so many young people today, he had been taught the humanistic notion that humans are adequate for their own needs.

"Please consider the alternative way of life your son has found," I urged, handing him a small booklet that shows how to become a Christian. We both agreed that it is sometimes embarrassing for us parents to have our children teach us things about life that we should have taught them. To be instructed by a young son or daughter can be humiliating. Somewhere along the line this very smart man had missed it spiritually. Even now, in his middle years, he seemed defensive and resistant about yielding to Christ. This good man's parents had not challenged him in early life to believe and trust in God. Were his son and I the first to share Christ with him?

Some parents say they do not want to influence their children's religious beliefs and will allow them to decide for themselves when they grow up. But this is an irresponsible attitude. After all, these same parents *do* choose to influence their youngsters' activities, choice of friends, education, clothing, and manners, so why should they shirk the responsibility to influence spiritual beliefs? Are they bending to the will of certain psychologists who consider it best that children be open-minded and think for themselves on issues?

On the wall of one probation officer's counseling room in a Georgia juvenile jail, I read:

17

Parents go to a lot of trouble to see that their kids DON'T learn certain patterns of behavior. Why not expend that much energy on what you DO want your child to learn ABOUT GOD. Only God changes people. Kids who come in here need changing!

That makes sense. Bible-taught people are wise. They can learn to deal with crises in a more positive way. Those who understand God's Word know how to reject or accept life as it comes along, and controversial subjects such as evolution, abortion, homosexuality, AIDS, and the meaning of life and death can be evaluated in definite terms.

Fortunately, a child can be rightly directed. Parents should be encouraged by the fact that kids often have fourteen-karat faith. They usually believe without questioning and seldom complicate faith with doubt. It is wonderful to observe that almost without exception, young children who are told about God's love on the Cross accept it in innocent faith, unmixed with argument. What a blessing to see a secure youngster who knows that God goes everywhere with him! He senses order and constancy in life. He knows he is loved and understands that God is a source of help. Take heart! There really *are* children like that in Christian homes today.

But even regular Sunday school training does not get this kind of religious education job done. Forty-five minutes a week just is not enough time to develop a working knowledge of the Christian faith. Nor is it sufficient time for producing confident people with high moral standards, people with enough biblical knowledge to know why they are on earth, how to love themselves and others, and how to live boldly without being a slave to fear. Furthermore, children who are placed in a church's program often are uprooted because a parent's job calls for a move. For instance, I know a military wife, mother of five, who says her family has moved twenty-eight times in her husband's thirty-three-year army career.

Some children attend Sunday school only sporadically at best because their attendance conforms necessarily to the parents' weekend work schedules. Many nurses, waitresses, maintenance people, store clerks, and others simply cannot attend church regularly. So it must be the parents' priority and responsibility to teach children about God at home. Moms and dads who are depending on the church, the pastor, the Sunday school teacher, or fate to get the job done are surely building on quicksand. True, some adolescents who have been spiritually well-reared begin to question the faith and wander away in teen years, but at least they know God is there and they have a spiritual nest to come back to when they feel the need. Remember the prodigal son and his return home to a loving, godly family (Luke 15)?

Kids really do need God! They depend on us adults in their lives to teach Bible truths. But we parents must teach these truths while the children are young because by adolescence, many youngsters are no longer open to spiritual truth or even to attending church. Many pastors tell me that the chances of an adult turning to Christ are even smaller.

It is difficult for youngsters to believe in a God

19

they cannot see or touch. Maybe the hundreds of suggestions in the next few chapters, ideas used successfully by others, can help you to light a child's life and pass on the good news that there really is a caring, loving God who will "father" us through life and even through death. These ideas have worked for others. They can work for you and your child too.

CHAPTER 2

Your Child and the Bible

O God, You have taught me from my youth;
And to this day I declare Your wondrous works.
Now also when I am old and grayheaded,
O God, do not forsake me,
Until I declare Your strength to this generation,
Your power to everyone who is to come.
                    —David, in Psalm 71:17-18

Children are little lexicons of humorous misinformation about the Bible and religion. One of ours, now grown, told me recently that for years when the Sunday school teacher read about idol worshipers in the Old Testament, she thought he was talking about lazy folks who stayed home from church on Sunday mornings. This same exuberant little girl stood up on the pew beside me in Sunday school singing her heart out at the top of her lungs, "I love to go to Sunday school, I love to sing a song; I hate to see a bacon [vacant] pew, I know there's something wrong . . ." Why not? The smell of breakfast bacon an hour before was still fresh in her lively five-year-old mind.

By the time she was seven my daughter was asking some sobering questions about the faith like, "Mom, do I really have to love Wendy today? She took my best doll home with her." At Christmas, precocious April was stubbornly telling her father, "Dad, I don't want to give part of my allowance to the church or to poor people either. It doesn't make *me* feel better to give than to receive!"

At first glance, the Bible's standards may seem wild and unrealistic; its stories, fantastic; its instructions, outrageous. No one, children included, who seldom reads it can be expected to believe the Bible. Its rules do not indulge the natural inclinations of twentieth-century people:

Love your enemy.
Pray for those who misuse you.
Turn the other cheek.
It is better to give than to receive.

You shall not commit adultery.
Love your father and your mother.
If you want to be great, be a servant of the rest.

But daily Bible reading with its constant exposure to God's rules likely will bring understanding, belief in its reasonableness, and commitment to its truths. For our leader, Jesus Christ, really did know what He was talking about when He laid out God's blueprint for life.

It is sometimes difficult to lure a child into a book that is twenty centuries old, much less to convince him or her that anything or anyone could really be the same yesterday, today, and forever.

Children have no eagerness to maintain the past. They sense the staggering swiftness of the world's progress. As planes fly two thousand miles per hour overhead, kindergartners are mastering basic computer skills. And high technology promises new possibilities with each passing day.

Nevertheless, the inescapable calling of parents is to lead their sons and daughters into the Book of books early in life. Today's children must somehow be taught that while the world changes, God does not. They must be led to seek the guidance, instruction, and unchanging truth that transcend time and transform lives. They must see Scripture as their own precious heritage.

SO MANY BIBLE CHOICES!

So much to do and parents seem to have so little time. How to begin? Let's talk first about choosing a Bible for your child. How can a parent know which version is best when some large bookstores may carry as many as two hundred separate versions?

There are many choices in an English-language Bible. Some versions were first published centuries ago; some are just completed. Some are shirt-pocket size; others are large with oversize print. Some have traditional black covers; others have denim or brightly colored covers. There is even a three-hole-punched notebook edition with wide empty margins for personal notes.

But the most important consideration in a Bible purchase for your child is not size or color but the translation or version you select. If your family attends church and Sunday school regularly, you are probably accustomed to using one version more than others. While the King James Bible is the best known (a 350-year-old translation), some people feel it is too difficult for children to understand. Even some adults I know get discouraged trying to decipher certain parts.

So other translations have appeared on the market. Although they are easier to understand, scholars differ among themselves as to which is the most accurate. The Revised Standard Version (1952) is not well received among many evangelicals. The New American Standard Bible (1963) is more readily received and maintains some of the majesty of the King James Version but with updated language. The New International Version (1973) is acceptable to evangelicals, employs modern language, and has been hailed as a highly reliable translation. One of the best and most recent translations is the New King James Version (1982), which also retains some of the majesty of the King James but does it in readable, everyday language.

The Living Bible has helped millions of people to unravel Scripture because its language is as up-to-date and modern as any book on the library shelf. Kenneth Taylor, author of the popular edition, makes no claims for extreme accuracy in its finest phrasing, but for the lay reader, the vital main themes are kept intact. It should be noted, however, that The Living Bible is a loose paraphrase that restates or rephrases an interpretation of the Bible; it is not a word-for-word translation from the ancient languages of Scripture.

But no matter which version you give to your child, the answers to human problems are likely to remain locked between its covers unless you, as a parent, personally take the responsibility to instruct him or her in the teachings of God's holy Word: "All Scripture is given by inspiration of God, and is profitable for doctrine, for reproof, for correction, for instruction in righteousness, that the man of God may be complete, thoroughly equipped for every good work" (2 Tim. 3:16–17).

GETTING STARTED

The Bible can make a dynamic difference in any child's life. Debra Allen writes in *Decision* magazine, "During our daughter's first year of public school after four years in Christian schools, we found the book of Daniel to be an encouragement.

Daniel's godly responses to a drastically new life-style and to people who did not know the true God helped Carrie Anne adjust to her own situation. No longer was Daniel simply a figure in a Bible story; instead, he became an example, teaching her how to relate to unbelievers, to acknowledge that God is the source of her abilities, to please God rather than people, to pray in times of difficulty and to realize that difficulties can be arenas of spiritual warfare" (June 1989, 24.) Allen clearly expresses our motivation as parents and teachers, but it takes both ingenuity and creativity to get kids to absorb enough Scripture to help them put their faith to work.

No project ever gets off the ground without a master plan. So, first of all . . .

1. *Read a good book about the Bible.* Get a little background yourself. There is much to learn about God's Word, and the more information you have, the better you will understand its messages so you can apply Scripture to your own life and relate it to your child. Although many excellent books are available on a variety of topics—for example, Bible geology, archaeology, customs, and interpretation—the sources listed at the end of this book in the bibliography under the heading "On the Bible and Basic Christianity" are helpful places to begin.

2. *Give a Bible to your youngster as a gift.* One wise mom I know marked key verses with a yellow marking pen. When her daughter Jenny received the book, the "landmark" verses stood out plainly and were the first and most often perused. Jenny was also given a marking pen of her own to continue coloring in her favorite verses over the years ahead.

3. *Help your child become familiar with the new Bible.* No one would dream of taking a child to a public library and assuming he or she would learn to use it all alone. Leaving a child unattended in God's library of sixty-six books is not good common sense either. Plan for some uninterrupted time, and leaf through the new Bible together. Show your children how to find their way around God's Word. Point out the Old and New Testaments. Count the books in each. Demonstrate how a written reference leads directly to a specific passage. Look up favorite stories and find old friends—David and Goliath, the wise men in the Christmas story, Daniel in the lions' den.

Of course, these exercises assume that you can find your way around the Bible. If you can't, perhaps you can request that your church offer an elective in Sunday school or on Sunday evenings for Bible beginners. You can also drop your pride and order early learning material that shows how to become better acquainted with the Bible. Broadman Press offers *Bible Guidebook* by William N. McElrath. Topics include what the Bible is, how to read it, how to use Bible helps, and what the Bible books are. Abingdon publishes *Finding Your Way Through the Bible* by Paul B. Maves which teaches how to look up references, finding books, chapters, and verses. From Gospel Light Press, *What the Bible Is All About for Young Explorers* by Frances Blankenbaker, provides an illustrated overview of the Bible. All of these books would be ideal to read together with children, and you could learn too.

4. *Motivate your child to study God's Word.* In-

clude with the Bible an extra surprise—a sealed envelope containing a message like this one: "Look in the den closet for a package with your name on it. You may open the package after you have recited the names of the books of the Old Testament perfectly to any adult in the family. Then look in the top dresser drawer for another surprise." Have a smaller box, just as carefully and intriguingly wrapped there. The card on it might say, "You may open this box after you have recited the names of all the New Testament books."

You might want to try a simpler plan. You could include with the Bible a "Books of the Bible" bookmark, puzzle, or ruler as a starter and offer a reward for every six names of the books of the Bible memorized.

5. *Purchase one of the following Bible promises books* for kids and help your child begin to claim a few to cope with special problems or happy happenings: *The Bible Tells Me So: God's Promises for Kids* compiled by Merla F. Hammack and Lisa Williams (Shaw); *Promises for Kids from the Book* (Tyndale).

6. *And finally, don't stop now!* You've only just begun. You've opened the door to sharing your faith and God's great truths with your child. Now follow through by picking one or two Bible learning activities from the list below that you and your child will enjoy. When interest in one activity wanes, choose another, then another over the months ahead.

SUGGESTED GET-ACQUAINTED ACTIVITIES

Select-a-Verse

Stuff an envelope or empty recipe box with about fifty file cards with a favorite Scripture reading typed on each. Let your child have the fun of drawing one each night before bed and reading it aloud. David C. Cook offers *Our Daily Bread*, a box shaped like a tiny loaf which holds 120 colorful cards with 240 Scripture promises.

How We Got Our Bibles

Show your child a copy of the book *The Dead Sea Scrolls and the Bible* by Charles F. Pfeiffer (Baker), which contains pictures and the story of ancient Bible texts. Or use a pictorial Bible almanac. Talk about how God spoke to many men and how they wrote what God said on rolled-up pieces of parchment. Explain the wonder of so many writers living so far apart in time and space, yet all writing the same message from God. And finally, talk about how God has miraculously preserved His Word through the centuries. A good story to look up and read in Jeremiah 36 tells of a wicked king who tried to destroy God's Word but couldn't.

What Do I Read When I'm . . . ?

Help your child copy this list onto a blank page of his or her new Bible.

What do I read when I'm	Psalm 42:5
sad?	Psalm 43:5
	Habakkuk 3:17–19

What do I read when I'm happy?	Psalm 33:20–21 Psalm 106:3 Psalm 104:33–35
What do I read when I'm lonesome?	Psalm 54:4 John 14:15–18 Romans 8:38–39
What do I read when I'm bored?	Psalm 17:15
What do I read when I'm discouraged?	Romans 8:28 1 Corinthians 2:9 Isaiah 43:2
What do I read when I'm feeling guilty?	Romans 3:20–24,27–28 Ecclesiastes 7:20 1 John 1:8–9
What do I read when I'm feeling hurt?	1 Peter 3:15–18 Psalm 18:2 John 16:33b
What do I read when I am tempted to do wrong?	1 Corinthians 10:13b 1 Thessalonians 3:4–6 Ephesians 6:11–18 Matthew 26:41 Hebrews 2:18
What do I read when I feel afraid?	Luke 12:25 Psalm 56:8–9 Hebrews 13:6–8 Psalm 121:1–6

Prophecy and Fulfillment

To point out Jesus in the Old Testament as well as in the New, talk about the Old Testament writers who predicted events in Jesus' life, then look up the corresponding passages in the New Testament where the predicted events came true.

Prophecy	OT Reference	Fulfillment
Born in Bethlehem	Micah 5:2	Matthew 2:1
Miracles	Isaiah 35:5–6	Mark 7:33–35 Matthew 9:32,33,35
Betrayal	Psalm 41:9	John 13:21
Beaten and spit on	Isaiah 50:6	Matthew 26:67
Resurrection	Psalm 16:10	Acts 2:31

Scribble Wall

Post a large sheet of colored plastic or oilcloth on a wall of your child's room. Have an understanding that everything that goes on it must relate somehow to the Bible. Provide water-soluble, nontoxic markers and a damp wiping cloth. Keep the scribble sheet active by suggesting fun after-school, Bible-related activities. Stimulate two-way communication. Here are a few examples:

Did you know Stephen was stoned to death? See Acts 6:8–15 and Acts 7:54–60.

Who is the world's oldest man? Write his name here: _____ How long did he live? _____ Where did he live? _____ (See Genesis 5.)

The sun stopped once. Read about it in Joshua 10. Write below in ten words or less what happened.

Which Bible story shall we read before bed tonight? Write the reference on paper and tape it to your bedroom door before 8 P.M.

I love you. See note under salt shaker for a way to earn

an extra cupcake. (Note says, "Any time before Saturday night, you may take a cupcake from the freezer when you can say the names of the books of the New Testament perfectly.")

EXTRA!!! Christ will return to earth one day. Read all about it in Matthew 24, 1 Thessalonians 5:1–10, and Revelation 19:11–16.

Surprise Treats

Occasionally put a note on the cookie jar (or any other appropriate place) that says, "Two free cookies at any time today for anyone who has read the Bible for at least ten minutes" or "A quarter for anyone who can recite 2 new Bible verses tomorrow."

Check-off Poster

Make a reading schedule of verses or chapters with rewards marked off at different intervals. Post the schedule in your children's rooms, and let them check off each passage as they read it. A "grand finale" treat might be lunch at McDonald's.

Bible Activity Box

An activity box is a tool to get kids learning by themselves. It is one of the best ways available to inject some Bible into youngsters while they are having fun. A Bible Activity Box is really a grab bag of assignments for children to work on alone.

To make an activity box, buy twenty large manila envelopes. Number each envelope and place a secret assignment along with a reward for completion inside each. Stand the envelopes on end in a cardboard box. Let your child draw one envelope, complete the assignment, and earn the reward on his or her own.

The activity box does not require a hovering parent. Somehow, the idea of choosing to do secret assignments apart from parental suggestion or coercion is intriguing to kids. And the box promotes positive attitudes about working with Scripture because each association with the Bible is fun and yields plenty of quick rewards. Below are eleven possibilities for envelope contents. Others can be easily contrived to fit your child's personality and preferences.

---

1. Enclose a piece of paper that says: "Set the timer for fifteen minutes. See if you can memorize Psalm 23:1–3 in that time. Recite to Mom and ask for super-duper treat."

2. Write one letter of the alphabet on each page of a small notebook. Ask the child to write the books of the Bible that begin with each letter on the appropriate page. You might also ask for the page number the book begins on in his Bible.

3. Place a small magnifying glass in the envelope with the instructions, "Read the book of Titus, using this magnifying glass."

4. Put several colored sheets of paper in the envelope with these instructions: "Copy good, helpful Bible verses on six of your favorite colored sheets. Do you like popcorn while you work? See Mom."

5. Place these instructions in an envelope: "Read the story of creation (Genesis, chapters 1 and 2) or read about Noah (Genesis 6, 7, 8, and 9). Then draw a picture

showing as many details as you can. Two hugs for each authentic detail. Can you keep me hugging all evening?"

6. Put a small pen-size flashlight in one envelope with these instructions: "After dark, get in bed and read one of the exciting stories listed below."

Acts 27	Paul's shipwreck
Acts 12:1–20	Peter's escape from prison
1 Samuel 19 and 20	Jonathan saving David
Mark 6:1–56	Jesus feeding five thousand

7. Write on a sheet of paper, "Read any chapter of the Bible and tell what it is about. Ask Mom for the 'secret something' on the top shelf of her closet when you finish. No peeking allowed!"

8. Give these directions: "Make a Bible verse bookmark for Grandma. Put it in the pretty card in the dining room bureau, third drawer down, left side."

9. Enclose a Bible picture and these instructions: "Cut up the enclosed picture and make a puzzle. Put the puzzle back together and memorize the verse on the back. Look in Dad's old bathrobe pocket for red scissors, jumbo pencil, and brand new tablet to work with."

10. Instructions for this envelope could read: "Make a Bible verse picture to hang on the cupboard door. Extra bonus if it contains at least twenty-five words and if you memorize the verse. Must be neat!"

11. Make up a book of coupons and staple them together. The coupons can say things like:

"This coupon good for six and 7/8 cents when you can say John 3:16. Want more? Try memorizing Psalm 40:17 and Hebrews 4:13."

"This coupon good for your choice of fruit, or a secret story about once when Dad got spanked,

when you have read John 1:1–29. Caution: This coupon is only good during months that begin with the letters, J, A, F, or D!"

"This coupon good for double allowance when you have read Matthew, Mark, Luke, or John all the way through."

"This coupon good for one free room cleaning after you read the whole book of John in seven days or less. (Let Mom know the day you begin reading.)"

SUPPORTIVE ACTIVITIES

By adolescence, youngsters ought to have established a daily pattern of private Bible reading and prayer and be as familiar with the Book of books as they are with the dictionary. It is, after all, their handbook for successful Christian living. Many varied activities will insure continued interest in the Word of God. Listed below are several Bible-related activities to help you meet this constant need.

Bible Correspondence Courses

Many ministries have excellent graded children's correspondence studies. Most ask only for a donation. Shortly after giving my daughter her new Bible, I wrote to the Billy Graham Follow-Up Department and asked that Gale be enrolled in their children's home Bible study course, *Trusting Jesus*. A few days later, a beautiful little study booklet came in the mail. Gale eagerly used her new Bible to fill in the blanks and sent the first lesson back, knowing she would get more mail in return. Her lesson was checked and sent back to her even before she got Lesson #2 sent along. For several weeks, Gale enthusiastically pursued her self-help journey into Scripture. The best part was that it took no daily pushing from me. The pre-planning was enough. She wanted to do it by herself in spare moments and most often picked it up when she was bored. Her motivation was the new Bible, a smidgen of knowledge about it, and a brightly colored Billy Graham study guide. Here are just a few of the ministries who offer this type of service:

Billy Graham, Follow-Up Department, P.O. Box 779, Minneapolis, MN 55440

Children's Bible Hour, P.O. Box 1, Grand Rapids, MI 49501

Emmaus Correspondence School, 2570 Asbury Road, Dubuque, IA 52001

Mailbox Bible Club, BCM International, 237 Fairfield Avenue, Upper Darby, PA 19082

Source of Light Ministries, 1011 Mission Road, Madison, GA 30650-9399.

Bible Clubs

You might want to consider sponsoring a weekly after-school or Saturday Bible Club. In many areas both Child Evangelism Fellowship (P.O. Box 348, Warrenton, MO 63383) and Mailbox Bible Club have trained teachers who will come by invitation to a home to teach neighborhood children about

Christ. (Look in the phone book for their number in your area.) They usually ask nothing but that you provide a garage, basement, or den and perhaps a few cookies and Kool-Aid for the weekly meetings. Their materials include a wide range of flannel-graph stories, books, songs, and Bible memory programs. And their teachers know exactly how to have fun with kids while recognizing their serious purpose of Bible study. Usually kids will flock to the sessions. Sponsoring a Bible Club in your home would not only be an effective outreach ministry, but it would also provide a routine, supplemental ministry for your own child. Perhaps you would enjoy a teacher training program.

Cupboard Door Christianity

Keep a constant round of new things posted on the cupboard or refrigerator door. Quotes from the Bible or well-known Christian leaders, human interest items, and cartoons all work well. As long as you keep changing them, your family will keep noticing.

Children's Publications

Freida was the mother of seven- and eight-year-olds. Both children were having trouble learning to read. The teacher had assigned them to read "just anything" they could for nightly practice. So Freida ordered a regular subscription of graded Sunday school papers sent to the house. They included crosswords, comics, cartoons, jokes, Bible-related stories, and fiction just right for each child's reading level. And the subscription did double duty. The kids absorbed the Bible knowledge willingly and practiced reading at the same time. David C. Cook Company will send papers quarterly for about eight dollars a year, including postage.

Anyone can subscribe to Sunday school papers. They provide cheap, profitable reading, are always interesting, and are graded from kindergarten through high school. The papers are usually shipped once a quarter and are inexpensive. And the kids love getting their own mail!

Here is a list of children's fun-inspirational magazines.

Search
Mailbox Bible Club
237 Fairfield Avenue
Upper Darby, PA 19082

Clubhouse (ages eight through twelve)
Clubhouse, Jr. (ages seven and under)
Focus on the Family
Pomona, CA 91799

Pockets
The Upper Room
1908 Grand Avenue
Nashville, TN 37202

Kids!
820 North LaSalle Drive
Chicago, IL 60610

Audio/Visual Aids

Find alternative entertainment for kids. One mom says, "For six months we paid our children a

small allowance each day they did not watch tele-
vision. It worked! We provided them with Christian
videos instead. The Bible came to life for them as
they viewed *The Amazing Book* (Multnomah).
They squealed with delight watching several
"McGee and Me" videos (Focus on the Family) fea-
turing state-of-the-art animation and realistic, sus-
penseful dramas. Christian bookstores carry a wide
variety of children's Bible story tapes, videos, and
records. On long trips cassettes are great for taming
kids—and adults! They also make good rainy-day
nap or bedtime companions.

Many church libraries have projectors and Bible
story filmstrips and videos available for check-out.
Our Mary Jo often had neighborhood kids sitting
cross-legged on the living room floor watching pictures flashed on a blank wall. She even named her
dolls Zechariah and Malachi after one such showing!

You can write for a cassette and video catalog
from one of these:

Inspirational Media
2700 Little Mountain Drive
P.O. Box 6046
San Bernardino, CA 92412

Kids International, Inc.
P.O. Box 35918
Tulsa, OK 74153

Tyndale House
336 Gunderson Drive
Wheaton, IL 60189

Cokesbury
P.O. Box 801
Nashville, TN 37202

Christian Tape Library
330 N. Range Line Road
Carmel, IN 46032

Word Books
5221 N. O'Connor Boulevard #1000
Irving, TX 75039

Gospel Light Publications
2300 Knoll Drive
Ventura, CA 93003

Flannelgraph is an effective reinforcer of Bible knowledge. Have your child retell favorite stories using flannelgraph characters. Children enjoy playing "teacher," gathering their smaller playmates around for a story. If a flannelboard is not available, suggest that they stick the figures on the back of an upholstered couch or chair. Borrow these from a Sunday school teacher or director of religious education, or look in Christian bookstores.

Bible Study Helps

Spark an early interest in Bible study. Acquaint your child at a young age with good Bible reference books. Photographs of Bible places, maps, and other helps can heighten interest in Bible study. It is up to the parent to provide the tools as the child becomes old enough and wise enough to use them. Intersperse new material at open points, and pray for

God's guidance and help in getting and keeping your child's interest focused upon the Word of God.

A concordance could be a wise gift for your child. Junior-aged kids love the grown-up feeling of being able to use a fat, difficult-looking book to find special information all by themselves. One Sunday morning, my nine-year-old grandson whined about Sunday school. He was delighted when I said, "Okay. You and I will have church at home." We reviewed the books of the Bible and the Lord's Prayer, and his eyes widened with interest as we read Scriptures about heaven and especially about streets of gold and no sickness there. I showed him how to locate other "heavenly" Scriptures in my fat concordance, and soon he was at it himself, rocking happily on the back porch glider, looking up, then locating and reading the verses long after I left him. The morning was worth a month of Sunday school sessions!

Be sure to purchase a concordance that matches the Bible version your child owns. Try playing "Scotland Yard" with your youngster. Give clues to a certain passage (perhaps two key words). Challenge your young detective to locate the Scripture you are thinking of, using the clues and the new concordance.

EMERGENCY SITUATIONS

Scripture (and prayer) can be a wonderful consolation for children as well as for adults. An emergency situation provides a good learning time. One of our girls began to worry about what would happen to her if her father and I both died. When her best friend's father died, the worry sessions increased. So April's daddy held her close in the rocker and said, "Our health is real good. You know how I can beat you in running and skating. We can take good care of you for a long time. But best of all, God goes on forever."

April sat quietly for a while, then said, "But I'm afraid to die too." Again her father answered, "God promised eternal life to all who believe in His Son. In this house we are all believers. You can trust God. When He says something, that settles it." Then he read to her from Romans 8:11 and John 3:16.

After the reading, April rocked quietly on his lap for a while. Then she said simply, "I think I'll go ride my bike now." Her worries had subsided. She had been well taught in the arms of a loving father about where to go for comfort in a time of need.

As you react to family emergencies, try to include demonstrations of faith in God and in His Word. Remember, actions speak louder than words. Show your children an active faith in emergency situations.

The Bible can be a wonderful consolation for children, just as it is for adults. Kids need to see it as God's loving guidebook rather than as a list of rules that take some of the fun from life, as they so often do. I told my daughters that the Bible is a book of directions something like the one that came attached to my new washer. When I ignored the maker's instructions and added too much soap, the machine couldn't purr happily along doing what it was meant to do. Instead, suds flooded up and over the top and spilled out underneath onto the floor, handicapping its purpose, sapping its vitality, and shortening its duration. Our enthusiasm about owning it was ruined for a while, too, as we all reluctantly cleaned up the mess. My children seemed to understand the correlation. Maybe that same illustration will help explain the Bible's purpose to your youngsters.

CHAPTER 3

You Can Teach Your Child to Pray

And it came to pass, as He was praying in a certain place, when He ceased, that one of His disciples said to Him, "Lord teach us to pray . . ."
—Luke 11:1

I asked bright-eyed Karlethia, a junior high homecoming queen who is also in my Sunday school class, how prayer had helped her single-parent family. At first she bit her lip and hesitated. She was remembering a rather tense situation when she insisted on a new "funky" haircut that had become popular among a few of her schoolmates, but her Mom thought too extreme. "I was mad when she said no," Karlethia admitted. "I pouted some and said some ugly things. Finally, Mom put her arm around me and asked if we could pray about it. That seemed okay, so we sat on the bed and Mom asked God to give me a right decision so I would make a good Christian witness among my school friends and that He would help me keep my faith through my teen years. She said she needed help, too, to make decisions about all of us three kids. Afterward, we hugged and after a while, the resentment was gone. I knew Mom only wanted the best for me." What a terrific way to settle a dispute—through prayer!

Six-year-old Eddy scrunched down in his little flowered sleeping bag where he "beds down" on the floor beside my big bed when he comes to visit his grammy. I heard sobs. Eddy's mom was very ill in the hospital. I crept out of my warm place and held him in my arms as I sat cross-legged on the floor, and we sang "Jesus Loves Me." Then I told Eddy that God really does hear and answer prayers, and I sang part of the little chorus titled "God Is So Good" to him, the part that goes "God answers prayer; He's so good to me." I felt Eddy relax in my arms and asked him if he wanted to talk to God and ask for healing for his mom. Lonesome little Eddy smiled. He garnered courage to pray aloud—for the first time, I think—just fourteen words, but so powerful amidst the tears. "God, you healed the blind man, so you can heal Mom too. Do it."

I tucked my precious grandson back into the sleeping bag. He fell asleep almost before I finished zipping it shut.

The testimony of a twenty-five-year-old man concerns the long-term usefulness of childhood prayer:

"When I saw my wife on drugs, senseless, first in a stupor, then mumbling, then shouting, then begging for help from imagined demons chasing her, then screaming, I was chilled with fear. What would I do? We were an hour off of the main trail up in the northern Georgia mountains. There was no one around for miles. So I told her we would pray. Neither of us knew how. She finally said she remembered a little prayer her mother had taught her. It was all we knew: 'Lord I am a sinner. Forgive me.' Somehow, it quieted us both to be in contact with God, even briefly. My wife relaxed there on the ground. I put my arms tight around her, and we went into a deep sleep, in midday with a grassy mud mound for a pillow. It was enough. God heard. He delivered us both from drugs right then."

Childhood prayers are not trivia. Good prayer habits taught to youngsters remain throughout adulthood. However, many adults responsible for training children feel confident without God and rarely talk to Him in prayer. When things are going well, we often do not seem to need God, and it is easy to forget to communicate with Him throughout the day. Many of us wait until a problem arises or until tragedy occurs before we disrupt our routines for a moment of prayer. Shame on us if we pass along to our children such a haphazard, unscriptural approach to prayer!

A routine prayer life is not acquired automatically with salvation. It develops through discipline, through an understanding of the privilege and power of prayer, and through exercising that privilege frequently. Once a parent establishes a regular prayer life, it will be easy to pass it along to the children. But even the disciples, who knew the Son of God personally, felt a lack. One asked, "Lord, teach us to pray" (Luke 11:1). And so we also should ask that He not only teach *us* to pray, but that He help us to teach our children to pray.

Here are some general principles to pass along to children of all ages. Some of these are discussed in greater detail later in the chapter.

---

1. Prayer is talking to God (Luke 11:2; Phil. 1:3–4; Eph. 3:14).
2. God hears our prayers (Ps. 116:1–2; 145:18–19; Jer. 29:12–13; 1 Peter 3:12; 1 John 5:14–15).
3. God answers our prayers (Isa. 65:24; Eph. 1:19–20).
4. We can pray any time (Ps. 55:1,16–17).
5. We can pray anywhere (Ps. 139:1–12; Jonah 2:1).
6. We can pray in any way—silently, out loud, short or long, in any position, in any language (Josh. 5:14; 1 Sam. 1:13; 1 Kings 8:22; 2 Chron. 6:13; Acts 20:36).
7. We can pray about anything (Heb. 4:16).
8. Prayer is not an option—it is a privilege, a responsi-

bility, and a command (Luke 18:1; 21:36; Eph. 6:18; 1 Thess. 5:17).

PRAYING WITH YOUR CHILDREN

Praying together over important matters can start early. Take, for instance, the example of a couple in New York State whose six-year-old was having problems in school. As the mother and I sat together over a late morning cup of coffee at the kitchen table, Robbie came into the room with his coat on. He was ready to leave for afternoon kindergarten. It was wonderful to watch Robbie's mom put her arm around the boy and pray with him about the day ahead. "Lord, you know Robbie has trouble sitting quietly," she said. "Calm him down today. Remind him often that he needs to stay in his seat. And keep his chatter down too. Miss Stone needs his help." Then she planted a king-size kiss on the child's cheek and sent him off to school with an attitude of "bring on the day!" The mother told me that they had been praying together daily for a month. And she showed me a note from the teacher telling of Robbie's improvement. What a lucky child!

Praying Any Time

The very best kind of prayer is spontaneous. A child ought to be able to listen to a grownup Christian whose prayer is simply a conversation with God. Children should realize that prayer is just talking to God, straight from the heart.

Have you ever stopped baking cookies or put down a hammer to pray with your child? That is how to teach a child to pray—when the opportunity presents itself. "Lord, we love You and know You watch us all the time and are interested in everything we do. Now help Daddy this afternoon as he goes to see the boss in the meeting. Put words in his mouth that will be just right. You can do that just fine, and we trust You for it. You know his job depends on it."

Or how about in the middle of the night when your child wakes up afraid? It may not be easy giving a lesson on prayer in the wee hours of the morning, but it will be an effective and invaluable lesson. You will have shown confidence in the Lord and His ability to help in a time of need. And how about after a disruptive argument? Or before school or before a trip to the doctor's office? How about when a beloved pet is lost or dying? The important thing is to show a child that God can always be reached at a moment's notice.

Praying Anywhere

Many people insist that absolute quiet is necessary for prayer. Quietness does promote reverence and clear minds, and we need times of quiet prayer (Ps. 46:10; Isa. 30:15). But quietness is not a prerequisite for prayer—and it's a good thing because silence is a premium commodity in our busy world.

Teach children that God can be reached from anywhere—a sun deck or a storm cellar; while swimming under water or flying above the clouds; in the velvet padded pew of a beautiful church or in a rickety folding chair in a half-constructed basement. God hears and answers prayers from anywhere in the world

Biblical Examples of Praying from Various Places	
2 Samuel 7:1–2,18–29	King David inside a tent
1 Kings 8:22	King Solomon inside the temple
1 Kings 18:19,36–37	Elijah on a mountain
1 Kings 19:4	Elijah under a tree
2 Kings 6:8–17	Elisha in the dark
Daniel 4:33–35	Nebuchadnezzer from a field
Jonah 2:1–9	Jonah from a fish's belly
Acts 16:13	Women by a river
Acts 16:23–25	Paul in prison

Praying in Any Way

We can pray in any way—silently, out loud, short or long, on our knees, on our heads (like one mischievous eight-year-old I know), or standing up. Many different methods and positions are illustrated in the Bible.

We can pray all by ourselves or take turns with another person. Large numbers of people can pray together by listening closely and silently, agreeing with what is being said. Even small children can learn early that they can help in group praying. To do this, they need to be told to pay attention and to think the same prayer thoughts as the adults. I heard a small child on her mother's lap in church utter "Yes, Lord Jesus" during a prayer for comfort for a bereaved family the child knew well. She had learned to consider herself an important part of the group. She felt responsible not to entertain wandering thoughts.

Biblical Examples of Praying in Different Ways	
Joshua 5:14	Joshua on his face before God
1 Samuel 1:13	Hannah praying silently
2 Chronicles 6:13	King Solomon kneeling
Matthew 26:39	Jesus lying on the ground
Luke 18:11–13	Pharisee using lots of words; publican using very few
Luke 23:46	Jesus with a loud voice
Daniel 2:17,18	Groups praying
Acts 12:5–17	

Praying About Anything

We should also teach children that anyone can pray to God about anything. Prayer is saying to God whatever is on your mind. Writer and teacher Dr. James T. Dyet illustrates this principle by using Hebrews 4:16 and this story: A primary Sunday school teacher asked her class for prayer requests. One little girl asked for prayer because she was apprehensive about spending the summer with her real mother. The teacher shied away from the broken home saying, "We don't pray about things like that." Another little boy was going to visit his grandparents. Grandpa's horse had bitten him earlier, so he wanted prayer that the horse would not bite him again. Once more the teacher replied, "We only pray about big things, not little things like that." And yet, Dr. Dyet instructs, the writer of Hebrews said to "come boldly before the throne of grace" (KJV), implying in the original text that we are to "speak our minds . . . to hold nothing back." Thank God for children who do not feel silly asking their heavenly Father for help—even if it just concerns a cranky old horse on Grandpa's farm!

TEACHING THE YOUNG CHILD

A mother who holds a young child on her lap and prays aloud teaches the child how to pray. The child sees her reverence, her closed eyes, her beseeching and sincere attitude. He or she notes that Mother speaks in ordinary language to her friend, God. A father who prays aloud before meals shows his family his faith in God. It may be that a four- or five-year-old will not understand all the words in family prayers, but much will be learned about the procedure of prayer.

But even a young child needs the opportunity and encouragement to pray—before any ideas of feeling silly or embarrassed have a chance to take root. To begin, the parent may have to put words in the mouth of a very young child. However, it is important to encourage youngsters to pray on their own as soon as they are able. And when that happens, let their words flow without comment even though the prayers may be bungling efforts and may sound funny to adult ears. One four-year-old thanked the Lord for the "roast beast" on the supper table! All his family said, "Amen."

Keep in mind that when Jesus said, "Let the little children come to Me, and do not forbid them" (Matt. 19:14), He no doubt was including their coming to Him in childhood prayer.

TEACHING OLDER CHILDREN

A helpful place to start is by reading Dr. Bill Bright's booklet, *How to Pray* (Campus Crusade for Christ). Dr. Bright suggests the A-C-T-S formula:

A-doration
C-onfession
T-hanksgiving
S-upplication

Discuss and practice these basic prayer principles using the guidelines in the rest of this chapter. You might want to hang the A-C-T-S letters up in your child's room as a reminder of this prayer process. Cut them from construction paper. Mount and frame them; or make a mobile. Refer to the A-C-T-S formula often as you pray with your child.

ADORATION

One edition of *Webster's New Collegiate Dictionary* defines adoration as the "act of paying honor to a divine being" or "homage paid to one held in high esteem." Obviously, in order to adore God, one must know He is worthy. So the first step in teaching adoration is to give children a reason to worship. They must begin to realize who God is, what He has already done for them, and what He has promised to do for those who love and serve Him.

Philosopher Thomas Carlyle wisely said, "Wonder is the basis of all worship." No one lives in a world of wonderment more than children. What an opportune time to introduce them to the wonders of their Savior and Lord! Begin to teach the attributes of God—not by hammering them into the child's memory one by one, but by commenting on God's great love or by pointing out His handiwork in creation or by exhibiting your confidence in His great power. Talk about the God who sees everyone everywhere all the time. Tell of the God who knows how many hairs are on each head; who designs every snowflake we sled through in winter; who calls each twinkling star at night by name.

Read Psalms 138, 139, 145–150; Job 38 and 39; and Ephesians 3:18 and 19. And then work some phrases—not sermons or treatises—of adoration into your prayers. Remember that children learn by example—examples that are clear and relevant to them:

"Lord, I'm glad You're God and that You can watch over me no matter where I am or what I'm doing."

"Father, I know that no one but You could make our roses smell so sweet."

"Lord, I thank You that You see me as a gift to You that You delight in. That makes me happy."

CONFESSION

Confession is the means to an effective prayer life. Many Scriptures indicate that God does not promise to hear the prayers of the iniquitous, let alone answer them (Ps. 66:17–20; John 9:31). But the prayers of a forgiven, righteous man unleash the unlimited power of God (Ps. 84:11; James 5:16; 1 John 3:21–22; 5:14–15).

If confession is the key, we need to understand exactly what confession is and practice it regularly. And more than that, we must instruct our children so that they too can experience productive, powerful prayer lives. To "confess" is to "say the same thing" about sin that God says or to take the same attitude toward sin that God takes. God hates sin and excludes it from His presence.

What is sin? Probably the best explanation for children is found in James 4:17. Sin is all the wrong things we do. And we should hate doing wrong and strive to exclude wrongdoing from our daily lives. But when we fail and do wrong, or sin, we should agree with God that what we did was wrong—sin— and ask His forgiveness. Psalm 51 is an excellent example of true confession. It shows David's abhorrence of his sin and the contrite spirit necessary for forgiveness.

Teach the principles of confession both by word and example. And teach that confession can be made anywhere and any time—in bed, at play, soaking in the tub, washing the car, or on your knees. A child should know that a person who confesses sin to God and repents of it is powerful because God listens to the prayers of a forgiven individual.

Most children will be reluctant to confess wrongdoing in your presence just as you would be hesitant to confess your faults in theirs! So have a time of silent, prayerful confession. Then help your child realize the love and forgiveness we experience as a result of confession. After the time of silent prayer, you might pray aloud: "God, I am clean before you. I have confessed my sin as far as I know it. You said You would forgive, and I believe it. I'll try not to do those wrong things anymore."

Even a child who confesses sin regularly can move the hands of God through prayer. God listens to the person made clean through the blood of Christ.

THANKSGIVING

Saying "thank you" is one of the first social graces we try to teach our children. But true thankfulness is more than just saying "thank you." True thankfulness and the expression of that gratitude spring from a realization that someone has done something for you. Thankfulness is an attitude (Ps. 9:1); saying "thank you" is one way to acknowledge a kindness or favor.

Psalm 50:14 says, "Offer to God thanksgiving . . . ." Hebrews 13:15 says, "By Him let us continually offer the sacrifice of praise to God, that is, the fruit of our lips, giving thanks to His name." Sacrifices are offerings, willingly given to God in recognition of His superiority. Sacrifices are not free, but require the offerer to give up something or to give of self. Why, then, would giving thanks be a "sacrifice"?

Most everyone has the experience sooner or later of attempting to evoke a "thank you" from a child. Perhaps a woman at a cash register offered your child a sucker. Johnny grabbed the sucker, popped it in his mouth, and headed for the door. You grabbed

Johnny, stopping him in his tracks, and said, "What do you tell this nice woman?" Nothing. "Can you tell her 'Thank you'?" you chided. Obviously not. After several attempts, *you* told her thank you and marched your child out the door to the tune of Lecture #247: "That checker was nice enough to give you a sucker. The least you could have done was tell her 'Thank you'!"

But for little Johnny to thank the lady would have required several things on his part—sacrifices, so to speak. First of all, he would have had to realize that she had done something nice for him. And probably he did. But in order for him to express his gratitude, he would have had to interrupt his sucker-sucking session, pull the candy out of his mouth, and exercise his vocal cords.

It might have been that Johnny didn't see any need to thank the woman. Perhaps he felt she *owed* him the sucker. Or maybe, since he didn't get the particular flavor he wanted, Johnny didn't see any need to be thankful. Or maybe Johnny didn't say "thank you" because it would have embarrassed him. And besides, why should he say "thank you" for such a little thing?

Although these are all invalid excuses and reflect an attitude of ingratitude, many children and adults are just as reluctant to offer thanks to God. We don't appreciate the many good things He gives us because we expect them; we feel God *owes* them to us. Or perhaps we are not quite as thankful as we should be because God failed to give us the particular kind of favor we wanted or because the kindness He bestowed upon us was just a little one. And it is difficult to interrupt our busy lives just to say "thank you." And maybe we fail to give thanks as we should because it involves a sacrifice of pride to bow before His throne and admit that He has done more for us than we could ever do for ourselves.

Teaching and nurturing true thankfulness then are not easy tasks. Thankfulness should be willingly offered to God as we recognize His supreme care for us. Try to practice finding things to give thanks for (Col. 3:17) all the time (Eph. 5:20), and encourage the same in the lives of your children. Be the leader in thanksgiving as Mattaniah was (Neh. 11:17). Set an example at mealtime as Jesus and Paul did (Mark 8:6; Acts 27:35), and also as David did (1 Chron. 16:7). Appoint others—your children included—to express thankfulness to the Lord. Giving thanks is a mind mender too. It is almost impossible for a gloomy attitude to prevail while God is being praised.

SUPPLICATION

Supplication is nearly automatic. Wanting and asking for things are natural. The hungry cry of a newborn or the grasping hand of a toddler are not learned habits—they are inborn traits. And "Gimme, gimme, gimme," is the battlecry of the whole human race, it seems.

But supplication is more than just asking. It is the act of making a sincere, humble request before God. It is based on our need and His ability to supply that need.

Jesus and the apostle John related supplication to

our familial relationship with our heavenly Father. A child has needs. A good father has both the responsibility and desire to meet the needs of his youngster as long as the requests do not interfere with that child's overall welfare.

John wrote that we become children of God through faith. Our loving Father hears our requests and meets our needs according to His will (1 John 5: 14–15). Jesus indicated that good earthly fathers give good things to their children, and because we know that, we should automatically expect our perfect heavenly Father to give us much better things in response to our requests (Matt. 7:7–11). When we know how much He loves us, it is almost automatic to turn to Him to ask for things needed and wanted. Use these verses to help teach the "asking for things" part of prayer: Ephesians 3:18–20; 6:18; Philippians 4:6; and James 4:2–3.

Finally, be mindful that a solid Christian of many years moves more and more toward enjoying praise and thanksgiving along with making prayer requests.

RESOURCE MATERIALS

For parents who want to learn more about the power of prayer and prayer procedure, read and apply the insight found in books listed in the bibliography under the category "On Prayer."

CHAPTER 4

Family Worship That Works

"... but as for me and my house, we will serve the LORD."

—Joshua, in Joshua 24:15

Children

Even when he's unaware, I listen
to my son's prayers of
love, innocence, adoration—
it's a good feeling.

Lord, how You must love
to hear him pray to You.
Lord, how You must long
to hear from all of us.
        —Stephen Jarrell Williams

There is unity in a family on its knees before God. Every member senses the presence of a higher authority. Humanistic self-reliance is left far behind when the overwhelming presence of God and His peace are felt. Touching elbows with other lives yielded to God helps reinforce allegiance to Him and to each other.

But unfortunately, many moms and dads resist routine family worship. To them, the idea suggests interminable Bible reading and lengthy prayer. They may have been unwilling audiences when they were children, and they remember unintelligible, adult-oriented "family altars."

Others deem family worship old-timey, boring, or ineffective. Some actually may have tried family worship for a while only to find the time more of an endurance test than an anticipated event.

Whatever the case, most parents agree that home is the prime learning place and worship is the spiritual force that binds a family together. Today's families need warm and close dimensions to face successfully a world of crumbling relationships.

A home devotional time offers parents a natural place to share scriptural truths and great Bible doctrines. Children can be taught to respond to God in faith with holiness and obedience. And with just a little planning, family worship can be intriguing enough to keep the whole family interested, learning, and worshiping. Creativity and ingenuity are the keys to successful home worship. Here are some challenging ideas to help you.

THE BEGINNER OR THE EXPERT

Maybe you're just thinking about beginning family worship in your home. Or maybe you've tried and failed. Or maybe you're an old hand at family devotions. Whatever your situation or level of expertise, attitude and expectations are important.

Be realistic. Unload the phony family altar image of superspiritual parents leading angelic cherubs in formal minichurch services at home. Kids are bound to whine when called in from play. Little hands will get into trouble when others' eyes are closed in prayer. Attention spans are sometimes short, and active minds tend to wander. Expect times of failure. But when they come, don't use them as an excuse for quitting. Accept them as typical, and begin to search for something new, something that will recapture interest. This chapter is filled with many ideas, tried and proved in ordinary family homes like yours.

Remember to pray specifically that the Holy

Spirit will work through your efforts so that the family will grow into Christian maturity. Ask often that He will speak to the needs of each individual and that each may draw from the daily worship experience what is lacking in his or her life for that day. Claim often the promise that He "is able to do exceedingly abundantly above all that we ask or think, according to the power that works in us" (Eph. 3:20).

If your family has not had a time of worship together before, introduce it gradually. Help your children enjoy devotions. It is, after all, a time in the day when they will have your full attention. Although it's not a play time, fresh, new, Bible-related materials and books can be included to make worship time varied and pleasant for all family members, regardless of age. Keep the worship time short. Stop while interest is high. Refuse to let family worship be grim or boring. (One family keeps a game of chess going from day to day as the group gathers!)

Family worship can be underplanned or overplanned, be too spontaneous or too contrived. It can be fun, inspirational, interesting, informative, or just plain dull, depending on the resourcefulness of the person in charge. Try to discover and use new and different ideas, materials—even times and places. And find out how other families make their worship time workable.

THE TIME

The gathering to worship will never happen without a plan. Choose a time when the family is unhurried and relaxed. Breakfast or dinner times have been traditional favorites, but with today's frantic schedules, other times may be more convenient. Occasionally duplicate sessions may be necessary to accommodate everyone.

Your family worship time will be riddled with as many—or as few—interruptions as you choose to allow. Most interferences can be handled quickly, postponed for a few minutes, or avoided altogether. Unplug the phone. Put the dog outside. Feed and change the baby. Send little ones to the bathroom before you begin. And let neighborhood playmates know that Johnny cannot play when the family has gathered. Anticipate problems and work around them. Make the small block of time scheduled for family worship the most important time of the day or week.

THE PLACE

Hold family devotions in various places for a pleasant change of scenery: on the back patio when the azaleas are in bloom, at the kitchen table, in the den or living room, in front of a glowing fireplace, in a circle on the rug, in a newly wallpapered room, on a porch swing watching a sunset, around one family member's sickbed, or in a boat on vacation. Let family members try to come up with different places to meet around the Word of God.

THE PROGRAM

The program and the methods of presenting the program should be as varied as the snowflakes in a winter storm. While having the same general content and goals, each gathering should be meaningful and interesting. The basic ingredients should be the same—worship, Bible-reading, Scripture memorization and prayer—but the garnishing should be spectacular! Kind of like your favorite oatmeal cookie recipe: the basic ingredients make it good, but the occasional additions of nuts or raisins or chocolate chips make it terrific! Read through the helps that follow and make the basic ingredients for your family worship good. Then throw in "something extra" from the section by that title and begin to reap the delicious blessings of successful family worship.

Basic Ingredient #1: Worship

Worship is praising, loving, responding in the heart to God; being in awe of who He is; being in a spirit of submission to His will. Worship focuses on God Himself. Thoughts are turned directly to Him in adoration, seeing God in all His wonder and worshiping Him because of it.

Worship is not automatic with children. The attitude of worship must be taught by example and cultivated through experience. Doling out information about God does not necessarily lead a child to worship. Nor does teaching a youngster to recite a list of the attributes of God ensure an attitude of worship. If there is no response in the heart, no wonder at who God is, the child is a long way from worshiping and loving the Lord with the entire heart, soul, and mind (Matt. 22:37).

Since worship is a personal response to God, family devotions should allow for and attempt to elicit this response from each participant. Teach, yes, but then ask for even the youngest child's reaction to our Maker. For example, tell the story of Stephen's martyrdom. Explain God's faithfulness to Stephen even through the terrible stoning. Tell how God gave Stephen a special glimpse of heaven before he died. Discuss God's faithfulness to your family. Ask each child to tell one special thing God has done for him or her or for the family. Then pray together, thanking God for His faithfulness and asking for the strength and courage to be as brave and faithful as Stephen was.

Each day let the children tell how the Bible lesson applies to their lives and how it makes them feel about God. Stories and other tools can be bland, sterile instruments of teaching, or they can stir up feelings that will result in worship and adoration of God.

Basic Ingredient #2: Bible Reading

Dr. Oswald J. Smith, former pastor of the People's Church in Toronto, Canada, says God's Word should be read daily just as manna was gathered daily. We would not dream of taking only one meal a day, much less per week, to nourish our bodies. So, he reminds us, our spiritual selves need regular feedings too.

Some families may prefer to start at Genesis 1:1 and read through the Bible. However, those I have known bog down at the book of Numbers with its long list of genealogies. Others may prefer to read through selected books. Acts, accompanied by maps, can be fascinating. The story of Ruth can be followed easily, as can the Gospel of John.

You might want to vary the reading. Sometimes read several chapters in sequence. Other times, choose verses on a single subject scattered throughout the Bible (use a concordance for help). Or use Scripture associated with upcoming Sunday school lessons. Every so often, have "favorites week" when family members share their favorite passages. Or for a while, pick Bible passages that quote Jesus directly. Use a red letter edition if you have one. Then ask the family to express in their own words just what Jesus said.

Vary methods too: let each family member take a turn reading on a given night; allow silent reading occasionally; let the parents read a verse, then the children; and so on. Alternately use a large-print Bible or any other favorite version. When a new translation is published, try it out. Provide yellow marking pens for individuals to underline parts of the Scripture that are especially inspirational or important.

And remember that no matter what plan or methods you are using, you are feeding young minds. Explain the tough places (like all the "begats"), define big words, clarify the basic ideas, and restate in ordinary language any difficult concepts. Just reading long paragraphs with big words won't get the job done. Make God's Word clear and usable to each person.

Basic Ingredient #3: Scripture Memorization

The mother of a nine-year-old tells this story:

"'I can't memorize all the Lord's Prayer. It's just too hard,' my Mark pouted one Saturday when I offered a new Nintendo game as a reward. The new game was Mark's fondest wish.

"'Yes, you can! You really can!' I insisted.

"All day, Mark ignored the bright green file card with the neatly typewritten verses I had propped up with a lollipop on the kitchen table. And all day, as Mark played with his cars and trucks on the floor while I baked bread, when we washed the car, and while we drove together to get groceries, I kept saying the lines over and over. In the late afternoon when we both grew tired and settled together on the couch, I repeated the words once more. Guess what? At bedtime, Mark was able to say nearly all of the Lord's Prayer along with me.

"Once he realized he could do it, motivation was high. Sunday morning, he was up early, and I found him curled up in his dad's big lounge chair before Sunday school, quietly working on the project. By Monday night, Mark was able to invite his best friend Andy over to play with his new Nintendo game. How delighted we were to realize that the Lord's Prayer had become a permanent part of our son's life!"

God commands in Deuteronomy 6:6–7a: "And these words which I command you today shall be in your heart; you shall teach them diligently to your children." Clearly, God's Word should be passed down from generation to generation in such a way that each generation knows it at least as well as the former generation. And a vital part of this knowledge is the committing of portions of Scripture to memory.

Psalm 1 and Joshua 1:8 tie the successful life and meditating on Scripture together. Since meditating means "mulling over, ruminating," or "chewing on," obviously the one who meditates on the Word must become thoroughly acquainted with it. Memorization achieves this kind of familiarity. So parents who want their children to become successful by God's standards would do well to help them memorize God's Word. Here are some ideas for building fun and interest into the discipline of memorizing Scripture.

• Purchase these books for great ideas to help in children's memory work: *Fun Ideas for Bible Memory* by Barbara Lockwood (Standard); *Memorizing Bible Verses with Games and Crafts* by Beth Short (David C. Cook) and *99 Fun Ideas for Teaching Bible Verses* by Elizabeth Crisci (Standard).

• Set up contests between adults and kids. Offer fun prizes. Draw up a "contract." For instance, "If the kids memorize the verses more quickly than the adults, the adults will take out the trash for a week. But if the adults memorize them first, the kids will do the supper cleanup for a week." Be sure to sign the contract to make it official!

• Help little children learn by repetition. Review while rocking, bathing, or playing with them. Repeat while driving or waiting in line at the grocery store. Here are some short verses one of our girls knew before age six:

- "God is love" (1 John 4:8).
- "For all have sinned" (Rom. 3:23).
- "Christ Jesus came into the world to save sinners" (1 Tim. 1:15).
- "Christ died for our sins" (1 Cor. 15:3).

- "I will give you rest" (Matt. 11:28).
- "Be kind to one another" (Eph. 4:32).
- "I and My Father are one" (John 10:30).
- "He cares for you" (1 Peter 5:7).

• Post current memory work on the refrigerator, closet door, or kitchen bulletin board. Or stretch a "clothesline," and clothespin verses for the month to it.

• Have memory charts. Award stickers, stars, or seals for each learned verse, prizes for every five stickers.

• Purchase a Scripture songbook, and sing Bible verses right into the minds of the family. Or make up your own music for favorite verses.

• Use flannelgraph letters or verse flashcards. Mix up letters and words, and take turns straightening them out.

• Write the verse on a chalkboard. Take turns erasing one word at a time. Repeat the whole verse after each erasure.

• Print different verses on 5x8 cards. Cut each card into pieces. Put the pieces for each verse in an envelope. Pass out the envelopes, and use a timer to see who can put the verse-puzzle together the most quickly. Have each member read his or her assembled verse.

• Let the leader begin quoting a verse, stopping after every few words to ask another person to add the next four words, or two words, and so on. Have a stick of gum or a lollipop ready for the first person to identify where the verse is located.

• Let the small children use magic markers to print the verse of the week on sheets of construction paper. Add stickers or magazine pictures and use for placemats at dinner.

• Give each youngster an empty photo album with see-through plastic pages. Insert weekly memory cards for an individual record of verses learned and for easy private review.

• Once in a while assign short Scripture verses to be memorized by the following day. Celebrate completion of the assignment with a yummy treat.

Several publishers offer convenient inexpensive memory packets. Navpress has *Well-Versed Kids,* a topical memory system with teacher manual to help explain the verses. Diadem Music offers *Hiding the Word Bible Memory System,* cassette tapes with entertaining sound effects and programmed repetitions to make memorizing easier. Word Publishers publishes the *Victory Scripture Memory Series* for teens and adults.

Basic Ingredient #4: Prayer

Prayer is vital to family devotions, so make prayer time meaningful. Keep prayers brief. Make certain they concern what is going on in family life and the world right then. Include requests, praise, and thanks. Pray in ordinary language, avoiding the archaic "Thee" and "Thou." If your family does not feel comfortable kneeling, don't kneel. Praying can be done in any position—out loud or silently—and children should know that.

Pray specifically. Avoid generalities. Rather than praying, "God, help Grandpa," ask God to give Grandpa the special patience he needs to get used to his new bifocals. Specific prayers are fervent prayers. And fervent prayers accomplish much (James 5:16). Such intimacy brings us closer to people, developing compassion and understanding of their problems. Some families enjoy keeping a prayer diary listing dates requests were made, new developments in situations being prayed about, items of praise, and answers to specific requests.

And remember, prayer time is not the time to lay out before God the shortcomings of other family members. Prayer time is not the time to sermonize. It is not a time to remind God that "Jack was a naughty boy today, Lord, so we need to pray for him!" Make prayer time a special time when hearts are united in love before the throne of grace.

Something Extra

Use these ideas to add extra sparkle to your family worship time. You'll find each helpful suggestion a delightful change of pace.

• Take turns acting out favorite Bible stories and let other family members guess the identity of the characters involved. Or use puppets. For extra fun, make a home video of the charades, and let the children invite their friends for a premier showing.

• End devotions with a popcorn party. Or have ingredients ready for do-it-yourself sundaes.

• Watch for terms in the Bible reading that lend themselves to dictionary research. Try to think on your child's level. (One of our daughters thought for years a "high priest" was a pastor on a very tall chair. An early introduction to a Bible dictionary would have cleared that up!) And remember to make "looking it up" in a concordance or commentary or on a Bible map a prestigious role.

• Begin worship time by alerting everyone that after the Bible reading each will be given the chance to stump someone else with a question from the text. Or ask a question or two before the Bible reading and have everyone listen for the answers. Or write questions poster-fashion and have everyone read silently to find the answers.

• Play Bible stories recorded by professional dramatists—Orson Welles or Ethel Barrett, for example, or look in your Christian bookstore for Bible videos. You will be surprised at the large number of choices.

• Adopt a missionary family. Read prayer letters from them, write answers to them, pray for them, and discuss ways to help meet their special needs. Need an address? Ask your church secretary for the name of a family supported by your denomination.

• If a session gets too long or complicated, excuse younger children for another activity—dot-to-dot Bible books, Bible puzzles, or a plastic Bible wall mural to color.

• Change worship time occasionally to coincide with a favorite religious radio or TV program. Or tape an especially good one for later use. Children's Bible Hour, P.O. Box 1, Grand Rapids, MI 49501 has an excellent kids' radio ministry on 605 stations. Write to this ministry for scheduling in your area.

• Begin by saying, "I am thinking of a verse in Genesis, chapter eight, that talks about a raven." Continue giving hints while the family members search in their Bibles for the correct verse. Have the winner read the verse plus the two verses before and after. For variety, sketch clues on chalkboard or paper.

• Memorize the books of the Bible. Number six envelopes from one to six. Print the names of the first eleven books of the Bible on envelope number one, the next eleven books on envelope number two, and so on. Then cut eleven shapes (stars, triangles, circles, and squares are fun) for each envelope. Write the name of each book on a shape, and put it in the appropriate envelope. Ask a child to put the shapes in envelope number one in order, using the list on the front. Scramble and repeat. When all eleven books from envelope number one are learned, move on to envelope number two, and so on, until all sixty-six books are learned.

• Use a tape series. Check with your pastor or Christian bookstore for interesting subjects available.

• Once in a while ask each child to come to devotions with something to share: a favorite Scripture, a poem about God, a record, song, or discussion idea. Encourage unusual presentations. One of our children brought a fresh rose and pointed out its marvelous yellow color, delightful odor, and the unique structure that God created.

• Use Sunday school papers. Read a favorite story or joke. (Incidentally, Sunday school papers and other Christian publications are terrific bathroom reading material!) One mother bought big notebooks for each of her children to store old Sunday school papers. She decoupaged the covers with pictures the children thought appropriate. Her kids know she considers the papers important. And the notebooks are often swapped to be read by others in the family.

• Bundle up in slickers, grab an umbrella, and go for a walk in God's rain. Take time to look around, to feel the droplets on your faces. Stop and wonder where they come from. Listen to the wind and watch the tree leaves tremble. Make patterns in the mud with your toes and talk about God. Wonder about how He makes the rain. Blow some dandelion fluff and remark about its beauty. Credit God with all of nature around you. And when you get home, share a cup of cocoa and Job 37.

• Watch newspaper ads for upcoming religious events. Many local churches advertise concerts, films, and plays they are presenting. Make a night of it. Dress up. Have dinner out before or after. And remember, half the fun is planning ahead and anticipating the special event.

• Talk about current events in light of the Bible. For instance, talk about Israel and the Arab nations. Tell children about Isaac and Ishmael. Show them how that blood feud is still going on between the Jews and the Arabs. Talk about God's future plans for the nations of the world. Build confidence by assuring children that God is in control of the whole world. Even wars and riots can be better understood and more easily accepted with the assurance that they are all part of God's plan.

• Relate or read an interesting true story of the faith. Missionary prayer letters and religious periodicals are good sources.

• Play gospel music. Instrumental and vocal selections are available for every musical taste from symphonic to country-western.

• Read the words of a favorite hymn aloud. Discuss what the author was trying to say. Find out something about the author if possible. The great hymns of the faith are our link to other generations who loved the Lord as we do.

• Devote an occasional worship time solely to singing. Take turns leading. Whistle through choruses, clap, sing in harmony or a cappella, or use harmonicas, piano, guitar or other instruments. One family used paper-covered combs and kazoos for a fun variation.

• Let children teach a new song they learned in Sunday school. Have them print the words out for the family ahead of time.

• Record the children's choir and play it back. Or use music as a quieter. Have soft music playing in the background while the family gathers for worship.

• Show the family a famous religious painting. Ask them to discuss what they think the artist had in mind. Ask how and why they would make it different if they were the artist. Compare what the picture portrays with what the Bible has to say.

• Have a Bible drill. The leader announces a Bible reference to be located by everyone. Bibles remain closed until he says, "Present Bibles." The first to locate the passage stands and reads it aloud.

• When one family member reads an inspirational book, allow time for it to be reviewed. Hopefully others will want to read it too. You might want to devote family worship time for a whole week to silent, individual reading of Christian books. See the suggested reading list at the end of this book.

• Make worship a thank-you celebration of family events. Celebrate graduations, birthdays, weddings, new babies, relatives visiting, upcoming vacation, completion of the new church wing, and so on. Relate the family affair to appropriate Scripture. Thank God in specific ways for each event. One family celebrated the purchase of a new home by thanking God for the money to buy it and for the freedom to choose it and by asking God's guidance in using it to His glory. They sang "Bless This House" and read Joshua 24:14-15.

• Buy or make puppets. Have one of the children tell a Bible story using the puppet. An animal puppet could tell an animal story—Noah's ark, Balaam's donkey, or Daniel in the lions' den. David C. Cook offers Winkie Bear teaching puppets and storybooks, and Accent Books has a book titled *Bible Puppet Scripts for Busy Teachers* by Diane Warner. *When Puppets Talk, People Listen* by Shelly Rodin and a series of scripts for building character and for use on holidays are available from Scripture Press.

• Families with teens will enjoy Serendipity materials, available at most Christian bookstores. Placemats are designed to help each member share some of the current significant events in his or her life. Especially useful is *Hassle*, a handbook for sixteen family relationship sessions.

• Invite a missionary family home on furlough to tell about their work. Ask a person with an especially intriguing personal testimony to come and share it with the family. Or ask your pastor or youth director to bring devotions one night.

• Plan a picnic. Delay family worship until you are all gathered on a blanket or around a picnic table.

• Use Family FunTime placemats imprinted

with tabletalk questions, family prayers, fun discussion ideas, and memory work. These are available from Sweet Publishing Company, 3934 Sandshell St., Fort Worth, TX 76137.

• Spend a few sessions reviewing the makeup of the Bible. Talk about how all sixty-six books fit together. There are many good visualized books on this subject. Some of the best to use with elementary school children are *The Bible: God's Wonderful Book* (BCM Publications); *What the Bible Is All About for Young Explorers*, by Frances Blankenbaker (Regal), and *Adventures Through the Bible*, a fifty-two-week study course for eight- through eleven-year-olds (Standard).

• Make up your own Bible quiz or pick up a book of quizzes. Christian bookstores carry many on various subjects and graded for all ages.

• Read rhythmically aloud and together some best-loved Psalms, the words to familiar hymns, or selections from the back of a hymnal as choral readings. For updated song lyrics, Hope Publishers has available Natalie Sleeth's *Adventures for the Soul*, thirty-five inspirational text poems from songs she records and the stories behind them. Kregel offers *101 Hymn Stories* (stories behind great church hymns) by Kenneth W. Osbeck.

• Spend several worship times discovering and learning how to use reference materials. Commentaries, concordances, Bible dictionaries, and atlases are all valuable Bible study tools. Many are available in easy-to-use-and-understand children's versions. Show how each is used and the type of information it contains. Then make assignments to be shared at later worship times. David C. Cook has Bible maps as well as time-lines and other teaching charts. In the bibliography under "Bible Reference Tools" are listed several suggested reference books.

• Write individual or group poems. One family uses the best of these for homemade Christmas and birthday cards.

• Study the Lord's Prayer or the Beatitudes, or read aloud Phillip W. Keller's *A Shepherd Looks at Psalm 23* (Zondervan). Children love to participate by making a scrapbook of pictures illustrating various passages.

• Let little ones have the regular responsibility of laying out the materials required for family worship.

• Tell about the person you had the most fun with today. Why do you think God allowed that person to be near you today? Read the story of Jonathan and David (1 Samuel 18, 19, and 20).

• Tell what you like about your family. Read Deuteronomy 6:1–2,5–9; Proverbs 1:7–9; 22:6; and Ephesians 6:1–4. Then praise God for the love, health, and unity of your family.

• Discuss how the Bible has helped you lately.

• Discuss what God is like and how we know about Him. Read Psalm 139, and Job 37, 38, and 39.

• Talk and pray about specific or pseudo-situations. For instance:

What shall we do about the neighbor's dog tromping down our garden?

How should Mary Jo handle her low math grade when she thinks she deserves a higher one?

If you knew your best friend was stealing, what would you do?

If you saw drugs being passed around at school, what would you do and why?

There is a mute, paralyzed person in the nursing home. How can we communicate and show our love?

Is war ever right?

How much should our family give to the church? Should we give to other organizations too?

What should we do about the neighbor kids who misuse toys?

What can we say to the children next door whose parents are divorcing?

• Make worship times around certain events extra special. Work in your own family traditions or use some of these ideas:

For *Christmas*, small children will love baking a birthday cake for Jesus. One grandmother joined the celebration by phoning a bakery long distance and ordering a cake. She sent Christmas plates, cups, and napkins in the mail. The family sang carols, read the Christmas story, lit the candle in the middle of the cake, and sang "Happy Birthday" to Jesus. The Child Evangelism Fellowship catalog lists a wonderful Christmas Party Kit and also seasonal visuals ideal for use during religious holidays.

For *New Year's Eve*, read Psalm 90:1–14 and 102:24–27. Sing "Another Year Is Dawning." Pass a "cup of blessing" around the table, each taking a sip from the common vessel and telling the best thing God brought into his or her life the past year. Sit in front of a glowing fireplace. Let the kids stay up as late as they can and hold the celebration as near midnight as possible. Share the happiest day of the year, the most disappointing, and the most satisfying. Afterward, light candles from the fireplace and sing "Blest Be the Tie That Binds."

For *Easter*, borrow Holy Land slides from your pastor or friends who have been there. Or borrow slides, a filmstrip, or a video depicting the death and resurrection of Jesus from your church library. Plant a tree to signify new life.

For a family member's *baptism*, borrow books or slides that explain its meaning. Read Scripture from Mark 1 or Romans 6. Discuss the baptismal service itself. *New Life for Boys and Girls* (Accent) is excellent follow-up material.

For *birthdays*, staple colored sheets of construction paper to white cardboard for use as placemats. After the meal, ask each family member to draw a wish for the life of the birthday person.

When your home is touched by the *death* of a close friend or relative, use the family worship time before the funeral to talk about God's marvelous provisions for Christians. Bring an unshelled peanut and use it as an object lesson. Talk about how the inside is more important than the outside (1 Sam. 16:7). Compare the empty shell to the empty body in the casket. Help little ones understand that the important part (the "inside" or the soul) is with Jesus; only the empty body is left behind. Use John 14 and 1 Thessalonians 4:13–18 or 1 Corinthians 15:51–58 for in-depth studies.

• One evening worship time, pass out paper and pencils. Have each person write down some good thoughts to begin the next day with. For thought primers, read aloud Isaiah 40:28–31; Psalm 90:1–2; or Psalm 118:24.

• Allow kids to work by themselves or in pairs for a week on a self-learning computer Bible program called *Baker Street Kids*, available from David C. Cook. Three levels of questions focus on recall, understanding, and discovery.

• Use a book of devotions written for families or for children. The list in the bibliography cites numerous other resources for creative family worship.

CHAPTER 5

How to Lead Your Child to Christ

Jesus said, "Let the little children come to Me, and do not forbid them; for of such is the kingdom of heaven."

—*Matthew 19:14*

Some parents assume their child is a Christian when it is not so. A child must make a personal decision for Christ. He or she must be told that eternal life is not inherited from parents and that there are no second generation Christians.

I have met only five mothers over the years who have personally led their own children to the Lord! Even in strong Bible-centered homes, parents sometimes skirt the issue with embarrassment. They seem to depend on the church to challenge their children to make a definite decision. Several pastors and Christian counselors I know agree that most people who do not accept Christ when they are children or young people never do so at all. The older people grow, the more they are fixed in their ways and the more difficult the decision becomes. Surely the children of believers ought to be believers too!

No parent has a right to rest until each youngster has made a commitment to the Lord. It is a high calling to lead a child from spiritual blindness into the light. It is a thrill to see a child possess with surety a title as a chosen person—adopted into God's family, planned for since God created the world, and loved as much as the Son of God Himself. Lead your child early to claim the crown and claim citizenship in the kingdom of God. Teach that belonging to God is sure because Christ has secured it. Assure him or her that a steadfast decision to follow Jesus is an inseparable and eternal link to God.

WHY LEAD CHILDREN
TO CHRIST?

Perhaps the key to fighting juvenile delinquency is the salvation of children before adolescence, for in the early teen years Satan wars mightily and successfully in their ranks. Once the job of evangelizing is done and the child's decision is made, the Holy Spirit will begin to direct the young life. Our God is the God of children, too, and will do far more than we ask or think. He provides an added measure of help through times of temptation and trouble. A Christian child has at least some awareness of the need for self-discipline. And if by adolescence he has had several years of training for Christ, he is more likely to make better life decisions and more choices that will honor God. The Holy Spirit living inside a youngster is not only a powerful leveler for that young person, but also a source of hope for frustrated parents.

It is pathetic to hear moms and dads crying out to God, in tears, for the salvation of disobedient teens. It would have been much easier to bring them to Christ earlier, and that would have allowed years at home to nurture their faith.

Presenting the gospel to children is significant business. We are dealing with human beings, not "just children." The conversion of an adult is no more important. Children have great potential to influence the world. God is watching. So are angels. And it is awesome to think that our sharing with youngsters is God's way of putting His plan into operation. It is God's way of ensuring that the children entrusted to us pass from spiritual death into new life in Christ. Long after contemporary buildings crumble and monuments erode, a child with his or her unlimited capabilities can be persuading others to believe. And it just may be that the door to bringing the world to its knees before Almighty God is child evangelism.

WHO CAN LEAD A CHILD TO CHRIST?

Almost anyone. It is far easier to approach youngsters with the gospel than adults. Kids are not nearly so critical. And kids are almost always willing to listen. They do not expect big words or high-powered knowledge, and they will respond positively more often than not.

What are the qualifications for sharing Christ with children? The purveyor of the gospel must be born again. He must have patience, a desire, and a method of sharing the Word. He must have a proper attitude, counting it a privilege to be an instrument of God. He must be dependent on the Holy Spirit to convict and convince the child of the truth.

As a Christian parent, you can claim your children for the Lord years ahead of their actual salvation experience. You can pray ceaselessly for God's power on behalf of your youngsters and their decisions for God. We do not work alone. As God's sons and daughters, we born-again moms and dads have the Holy Spirit's wisdom, power, and love to help us lead our kids to Christ. We can approach the subject of salvation with great surety and confidence, knowing the Holy Spirit will help us find just the right words to say. Remember that ultimately youngsters belong to Him, are returnable to Him, and that the Spirit's interest in seeing them saved is enormous. He will apply the truth of Scripture and open their minds to see the Savior. And He is the one who sets the timetable for conversion. This knowledge takes the pressure off the parent to press for a decision "today." As Bill Bright, a well-known Christian leader, says, "We share Christ in the power of the Holy Spirit and leave the results to God." We can trust the Holy Spirit's timing. If a child is not ready, the parent's job is to try again later, and perhaps even again, until the youngster fully understands and willingly accepts the claims of Christ upon his life.

The exciting fact is that when the job is done, we parents have then produced baby Christians! We need not necessarily go to the mission field for our converts. Through spiritual multiplication, our saved children sharing with *their* children could make us spiritual grandparents—or even great-grandparents—before we die!

WHEN CAN A CHILD BE LED TO CHRIST?

You can block a child's way to God by delaying his or her salvation. No place does the Bible set an appropriate age. Normally able to understand the gospel story very young, a child should not be denied the truths of God. Our school systems would have us believe that six years of age is the right time to begin formal teaching of children and that there is a correct age to introduce every item thereafter. Some say there is an "age of accountability" when a child knows right from wrong, and some have speculated that age is between eleven and thirteen years. Others believe a small youngster does not have the intelligence or wisdom to understand what accepting Christ means.

But do not be timid about presenting Christ early! Believing Christ for salvation should not be hard at all. The message of the gospel is simple. Kids understand love, so they understand Jesus. A child doesn't have to be very old to recognize and say, "God loves me." The message of John 3:16 can be comprehended by even a five-year-old. Children respond to love, and they too can see that giving up one's life for another is the highest form of caring. But there is more to salvation than realizing that "God is love." The child must also realize that everybody has done some wrong things and thought some bad thoughts, that sin is unacceptable to God because it hurts His children and that God sent His Son, Jesus, to die for sins. A child who has grasped these facts may then be ready to make a decision about Christ.

Entrance into God's kingdom is not complicated and does not depend on a wealth of wisdom, money, or anything else children do not have. Salvation is believing, and an unsophisticated child has more faith than many adults. Most children trust nearly everyone, so it is easy for them to trust Christ. There are no great theological depths to be explored and understood. Only a kid-sized bit of information is needed for salvation. Even adults have to be saved on children's terms, coming with a simple understanding and faith. Why, then, do we question that a child can come to Christ? The simple childlikeness is not a deterrent, but a natural channel to God for youngsters.

The new birth often occurs in the lives of six- to eight-year-olds. Many missionaries, pastors, and strong laypersons became believers very early. Believing does not require an adult mind, and we have no right to discourage a decision at any age.

After salvation, a child learns more and more about the choice to believe. The personal faith grows as the years go by. In vacation Bible school one summer, I taught the first graders a simple five-minute lesson on salvation and told them they would need to make a decision about Christ someday. I quietly asked that anyone ready now let me know privately afterward. One seven-year-old told me firmly that she had already prayed and received Christ into her life. She was absolutely sure.

If we tell our kids from the time they are very small that God is love, that Jesus died for them, and that believers belong to God, then it is perfectly natural to expect that they will be saved—possibly before the age of twelve. Didn't we dole out the gospel carefully in bedtime stories hoping for just that? Then why hinder a child's decision when he or she is ready? Let children come at the time of life when it is easiest of all. And when they make that decision, accept it as real. Our children's salvation should not arouse our suspicions. We should not doubt the authenticity of their response. They are the natural fruits of our teaching and the Holy Spirit's promised work.

Encourage the young believer. Show the assurance of his or her salvation in John 3:36; 6:37; 10:28; 2 Timothy 1:12; Titus 1:2; and 1 John 5:11–13. And tell the child, "Yes, if you believe that you have sinned and that Jesus died and rose again, you are saved forever. And no matter what else happens, when you die, you will go to live in heaven."

NO PUSHING, PLEASE

Watch for your child's readiness. Avoid manipulative techniques. And never press children to walk the church aisles. Some kids will "go forward" during an invitation at church just to gain attention or to do what they think is expected. Any human juggling apart from the Holy Spirit's influence accomplishes little.

Some youngsters can apply the plan of salvation faster than others—even others in the same family. You may faithfully lay a planned foundation of several years before a child seems ready to make a profession of faith. Or your child may need very little prompting before deciding to follow Christ. The parent's job is to present the claims of Christ clearly and often, directing, not driving, the child to Christ. And remember, children are not necessarily saved in the same order they were born. Younger children may receive Christ before older ones.

Matthew 13 tells the story of the sower of seeds. Some seeds fell on good ground, some in stony or thorny places. Children, with their accepting attitudes, are often the "good ground." But if they are not, don't get frantic. Present the gospel again a little bit later. Don't push. Try to remember that as a parent, you are simply the instrument for getting the message to the youngster at your knee. The Holy Spirit is responsible for the timing and results.

WHAT MUST A CHILD DO TO BE SAVED?

God does not dole out a child-type conversion to people under twelve and another to adults. The message and the process are the same for both. The child believes in exactly the same way as the adult. There are no tryout periods and no special concessions for the young. The gospel is simple enough for all to comprehend: all—men, women, and children—have sinned, and Jesus died for each one.

It is important not to talk down to the youngster. You are after a vital decision. Once you have prepared the way with the basic story, invite the child to accept Christ. It is easy simply to tell the story and stop. But that will not get the job done. God wants each little person you deal with to turn to Him. Tell the youngster that just knowing the facts is not enough and ask him to tell you his decision aloud. That will not be hard. Kids respond easily: "Do you believe all of this, Sue? Then let's pray and invite Christ into your life right now. Do you want to?"

I chose a rain-washed Saturday to share with one of our daughters. I find subtle beauty in rain splashing against windows and running fervently through the eaves. A dark day provides opportunity to enjoy indoor things. No little friends would knock on the door; nothing much was on afternoon TV to intrigue her; and going out to play held no allure since water overflowed the street curbs. Plainly, there was not much of anything to do. So Mary Jo listened attentively.

Once in a while a child will come to you and ask how to become a Christian. Perhaps a special Sunday school lesson or a book or message will prompt the question. More often, however, the parent will need to take the initiative. You could write a letter to the child as I did and post it on his or her bedroom door:

> Big doings at 4 P.M. in my room. Cookies and milk and important talk. Meet me there today.
>
> Love,
> Mom

Or you might say, "Let's sit together by ourselves in the den (porch swing, hammock). I have something important to talk to you about."

If you're not exactly sure how to begin the "important talk," try ordering the comic booklet *Good News* (Here's Life) or *A Child of God* (BCM Publications) to read together with your child. Each has a place where youngsters can fill in their names to personalize what Christ has done. Afterward, enroll your child in beginner children's Bible correspondence courses offered by Mailbox Bible Club, BCM Publications, 234 Fairfield Avenue, Upper Darby,

PA 19082, or Billy Graham, Minneapolis, MN 55403.

Scripture Press publishes an eleven-by-seventeen-inch, visualized chart titled, "How to Become God's Child." It explains in primary-age language what happens when a child receives Jesus and how to live as a member of God's family.

WHAT NOW THAT THE CHILD HAS RECEIVED CHRIST?

Pray for the child relentlessly. Prayer is a parent's secret service on behalf of a youngster. Depend on the Spirit to work daily. And encourage the child to tell others about his or her decision to follow Christ. Telling others will reinforce in the child's own mind that something important has happened. Go over the plan of salvation again and tell Jenny she can share Christ with someone else just as you shared with her.

Nurture discipleship. Help your child adopt an attitude of, "Okay, Lord, what do You want of me? I want to follow You; You are my leader."

Reinforce the assurance of salvation: "No matter how you feel, you can trust God's Word and what it says. You don't have to *feel* saved. God's Word says you belong to God because you believe Christ died for you. And whatever God's Word says is true. Some mornings you may wake up feeling really 'blah.' You may not *feel* saved. You may feel like God has disappeared. But you are still God's child on those days too. And God never disappears. He said He would never leave. Believe it."

A child's assurance of salvation usually comes more easily than an adult's. The simple childlike faith that brought the child to God also swings into action when extra faith is needed. Most kids just believe they are God's and that is that. They seem to have uncomplicated assurance of what God has done in their lives.

But what if a child wants to ask Christ into his or her life a second time? Don't panic. Reaffirm that once is enough. God keeps His promises. Read John 3:36; 6:37; 10:28; 2 Timothy 1:12; Titus 1:2; and 1 John 5:11–13. If you wish, you can then say, "Let's make it final once and for all right now, asking Christ in forever. Then you will never have to do it again."

Above all, be very much aware of the infinite value of the child and the child's decision. A child's salvation can be very real indeed and is of immeasurable worth, unfathomably important. God allows kids into His family, and we need to welcome them in also. An immortal spirit has determined its eternal destiny. A human being has begun to love the Lord with all his or her heart, soul, and mind. Spiritual beginnings are often frail and tender, but nonetheless valid and wonderful. Encourage the child in the faith by smiling on what he has done. And let him know you respect his decision as real.

Don't expect perfect behavior because of the youngster's conversion. Remember, only simple faith is needed to come to Christ (Eph. 2:8–9; Acts 16:31). Immediate perfect conduct is not required. Although a child of God is a new person (2 Cor. 5:17), he or she needs time to grow. Help by allow-ing for some stumbling and disobedience. And recognize each wonderful success along the Christian learning process.

A friend of mine tells the story of a retiring ship captain. For twenty-five years the men had respected his strictness and rigid authority, saluting every time they met him on deck. When he retired, a new captain came aboard, but the former captain remained a while to break him in. Despite the arrival of the new captain, the men sometimes found themselves saluting the old leader out of habit, even though they were beginning to respect the authority of the new. Breaking away from the old captain proved difficult and took time. Just so, when the new authority (the Holy Spirit) arrives in a new Christian's life, He must live side by side with the old nature. It takes a while before the new captain commands respect and obedience. But little by little the signs of growth will appear.

CHAPTER 6

When to Teach What

Whom will He teach knowledge?
And whom will He make to understand
  the message?
Those just weaned from milk?
Those just drawn from the breasts?
For precept must be upon precept,
  precept upon precept,
Line upon line, line upon line,
Here a little, there a little.
                    —Isaiah 28:9-10

Kids. They are filled with super energy, abounding in unlimited potential for absorbing new ideas about God. Making God's treasures available at just the right times in a child's life will build a solid foundation for Christian growth and experience.

Introducing abstract subjects like the meaning of baptism and communion will certainly not harm a child. Like saluting the flag, the young child at first will not fully appreciate the symbolism involved, but he or she will at least become familiar with the terminology and with the symbol itself. Later on, understanding will grow, and the true meaning will unfold. But too much too soon can cause confusion in the child and disappointment in the teacher. And a very young child subjected to a battery of vague, symbolic concepts may see religion as boring or incomprehensible. The child may even form incorrect, concrete notions that will need to be corrected and relearned at a later date. (For years I connected communion with lunch and magic with Christ's being everywhere.)

But the right ideas introduced at the right times will have far greater impact and will lay a better groundwork, enabling a child to have continuing exciting experiences with God.

That is the purpose of this chapter. It shows when to introduce what and is offered with the hope that moms and dads and teachers will use it with great sensitivity to the Holy Spirit's leading.

The following list of ideas has been gathered from a number of sources through my years of studying, teaching, speaking, and parenting. I wish I could remember and give proper credit to all those who helped me compile this list, but at this point I must be content with a public expression of appreciation. Thank you.

Now, please keep in mind that this chart serves only as a guideline; each youngster develops by a personal, internal clock, some comprehending difficult concepts earlier than others. You know your child better than anybody else. When you know your child is ready, teach!

15 Months to 3 Years

Characteristics:

Short attention span
Likes playing alone
Cannot form concepts
Quite restless
Is best taught alone, one-to-one, in brief sessions
Loves to be read to, loves pictures
Loves to be rocked and sung to

Can Learn These Bible Truths:

Children should obey their parents.
We go to church to learn about God.
God watches over me.
God made the world.
The Bible tells about God.
God loves me.

Can Master These Skills:

Saying a short prayer
Singing "Jesus Loves Me," "Away in a Manger," and other short songs

4 and 5 Years

Characteristics:

Very inquisitive
Full of energy
Growing fast
Believes everything
Loves to hear favorite stories over and over
Loves Jesus stories
Usually enjoys Sunday school
Sees Mother as very important

Can Learn These Bible Truths:

Jesus died for sin.
Jesus never leaves me.
God made everything.
God loves children.
God wants children to obey their parents.
God wants children to be kind and to share.
The Bible is important because it tells what God wants us to know.

Can Master This Skill:

Learning short verses by casual repetition
(The word "memorize" is not understood yet.)

6 to 8 Years

Characteristics:

Curious and active
Needs to be kept busy
Terrific imagination
Believes most of what he or she is told
Developing sense of right and wrong

Usually wants to please parents

Sensitive to approval or disapproval

Less self-centered now, developing some concern for others

Doing things with others more important now

Usually not ready to learn abstract concepts

Can usually read some, even a little from the Bible, with help

Prays, trying to get God to do things, regardless of His will

Loves interesting stories of Bible people

(Teach the lives of Jesus, Zaccheus, the Good Samaritan, Samuel, Eli, David.)

Can Learn These Bible Truths:

The Bible is true.

God is the Creator.

God sees all and is a powerful helper.

God loves everyone.

Jesus is the Son of God; Jesus was born, died, rose again, and is in heaven.

Everyone sins, and God is the only One who can forgive sin.

Everyone needs to accept Jesus as Savior.

(A few children will be ready to invite Christ into their lives at this age.)

The church is made up of people who believe in Jesus.

Heaven is for people who accept Jesus.

Satan is glad when people sin.

(For extra help, use *Devotions for the Children's Hour* by Kenneth Taylor [Moody] or *Leading Little Ones to God* by Marian M. Schoolland [Eerdmans].)

Can Master These Skills:

Using the Bible some

Beginning to learn the books of the Old and New Testaments

Memorizing passages of Scripture like the Twenty-third Psalm and the Lord's Prayer

---

9 to 12 Years

Characteristics:

Beginning to talk about his faith now

Ready to discuss how to apply truths

Likes to discover through research and learn new things

Attention span good

Slowing some in physical growth

Has great energy, loves to be on the move

Peer pressure growing

Likes working in groups

Often loud, competitive

Often likes history

Will often copy heroes from character/action stories

Can Learn These Bible Truths:

How the Bible came to us and its flawless character

God has a purpose for everyone's life.

Prayer is powerful.

God is majestic, awesome, holy.

The meanings of parables and other symbolic concepts in the Bible

How the local church functions and the jobs of its staff

About what other denominations believe, the danger of cults

Can Master These Skills:

Bible study

Giving

Witnessing

Putting some Christian service principles into action

---

13 to 16 Years

Characteristics:

Exposed to powerful peer pressure

Growing independent of parents

Thinking about a vocation

Abstract thinking now possible

Religious ideas possibly wavering from radical to rigid with great emotion

May question God

May come up with beliefs different from parents

Setting own individualized pace for physical, spiritual, and emotional development

Matures very fast, girls faster than boys

Gives less importance to home activities, more to outside activities

Needs love, understanding, sympathy, and stabilizing influences

Tries to understand life and develop an identity

Spends a lot of time thinking about God, life, death, and the "whys" of life

Understands what ethics are

Can Learn These Bible Truths:

The reliability of the Bible

The dependable, unchangeable, inalterable character of Jesus

The will of God

The ministries of the Holy Spirit (helper, guide, teacher, comforter.)

How to receive Christ personally and to share that faith with others

Church doctrines and their meanings
Church history, new movements in Christianity

Can Master These Skills:

Bible study
Lifestyle
Career
Using reference materials and methods of all types

Your child is special, unique, developing unlike any other. Watch, wait, and pray for the right time, the right place, to introduce the facts and the comforts of God's Word. Love will help you get the job done day by day.

CHAPTER 7

The Ten-Minutes-a-Day Reading Plan

Give us this day our daily bread.
—Jesus, in Matthew 6:11

It does not take great knowledge of Scripture to lead children into the Bible and along the doctrinal path. Soft organ music, stained glass windows, well-equipped Sunday school rooms, and long lectures are not required. All it takes is a concerned adult with a plan and determination. Some parents feel so inadequate that they avoid home Bible teaching. But there are no perfect parents to pass on the faith—only us—flawed as we are. God has used people just like us to preserve His divine rule ever since the days of Adam and Eve. We, then, must accept our responsibility to preserve it further by passing it on to our children and grandchildren.

This last chapter is designed to produce people with a faith stronger than that of the generation before: children better than ourselves. The simple strategy can begin at about age nine and requires only two to ten minutes daily. Just a short time each day is an invaluable investment in rocklike spiritual underpinnings to sustain the future adult for life. There is no teacher's manual. The Bible itself is the only essential tool. But moms and dads will be learning too, because every contact with the Word will help them as well as the kids.

An easy-to-understand paraphrase or translation of the Bible might be particularly appropriate for your child. For younger children, I recommend the Living Bible, for older youngsters, the New King James Version.

Here's how the plan works: Read a short passage each night. Scriptures are arranged topically. Each theme will be covered in depth, in some cases for two months. Each week, one verse is highlighted for nightly review and memorization if desired.

With this program, you and your youngster will read large portions of the Bible together. In one year, you will focus in detail on fifty-two verses. Little preparation is required because no comments are needed unless you desire to make some. The Bible readings can speak for themselves, and the Holy Spirit can do the teaching (John 16:13).

As you use this simple plan, your child will have daily contact with God's Word under a personal tutor. Children can develop a feel for the language of the Bible and begin to understand its makeup early in life so they are "at home" reading and studying it. By handling the Bible nightly, children will quickly learn the location of various books and how to locate specific references. And they will gain respect for the Bible as an authoritative source, seeing it as an instruction book for living, given by God Himself. Kids will learn early that the search for God's truth begins and ends in the Bible.

This approach is portable, and its concepts are transferable. Moving down the block or out of state or even going on vacation need make no difference in the nightly routine. The youngster's instruction can easily continue. The steady diet of one-topic Bible readings can go right on. Verses for emphasis can be put on cards and taken along. They can be posted on the refrigerator, the dashboard, or the motel room desk for convenient and casual review. And weekly verses can be shortened or lengthened according to a child's age and ability.

Here are fifteen months of nightly readings to get

started. When these are completed, any parent using a concordance can easily compile more topical listings. Single parents will find this plan useful. It's a time saver that works. After two or three years the assignments can be repeated for valuable review. Parents may need to adjust each suggested reading and memory verse up or down a line or two for clarity depending on which version of the Bible is used and how it reads.

Fifteen Months of Nightly Readings

Scripture Reading	Memory Verse
The Bible: Why It Was Written:	Hebrews 4:12
1. John 20:30–31	
2. Psalm 19:7–11	
3. 1 Timothy 3:14–17	
4. Hebrews 4:12	
Proverbs 1:33	
5. Psalm 119:9–10	
6. Psalm 119:96–105	
7. Deuteronomy 17:18–20	

Scripture Reading	Memory Verse
1. Matthew 4:4	2 Timothy 3:16
Romans 1:16–17	
2. 1 Peter 2:2–4	
3. John 5:39	
4. Romans 10:9–13	
5. Revelation 1:1–3	
6. James 1:21–25	
7. John 15:1–3	

Fifteen Months of Nightly Readings

Scripture Reading	*Memory Verse*
1. Isaiah 55:8–13	Psalm 119:105
2. Ephesians 6:13–18	
3. 1 John 5:13	
4. 2 Peter 1:19–21	
5. 1 Peter 1:10–13	
6. 1 Peter 1:23–25	

*The Bible: Its Writers
and How They
Viewed Their Jobs:*
7. Amos 7:14–16

---

1. 2 Samuel 23:1–2	2 Peter 1:20–21
2. Jeremiah 1:4–10	
3. Ezekiel 3:1–11	

*Understanding the
Bible; Wisdom:*
4. 1 Corinthians 2:14–16
5. John 14:15–17,26 (The
Holy Spirit is the key.)
6. John 16:13
7. 1 John 2:20,27

---

1. 1 Corinthians 2:7–10	Psalm 119:11
2. 1 Corinthians 2:11–13	
3. Psalm 119:11	
4. Psalm 119:12–17	
5. Psalm 119:18–19	
6. James 1:5–8	
7. Psalm 25:14	

Fifteen Months of Nightly Readings

Scripture Reading	Memory Verse
Prayer:	Psalm 34:15

Prayer:
1. Psalm 11:4,7
2. Psalm 34:15,17
3. Psalm 66:18
4. Psalm 130:1–6
5. Proverbs 28:9
6. 1 John 3:19–22
7. Isaiah 58:1–9

Psalm 34:15

---

1. Isaiah 59:1–9
2. John 15:7–17
3. Mark 11:24–25
4. 1 Peter 3:7–12

How to Pray:
5. Ephesians 6:18–20
6. Luke 11:5–10
7. Matthew 6:5–15

Psalm 66:18

---

1. Matthew 21:16
2. Colossians 4:2
   Philippians 4:6–7
3. 1 Samuel 12:23
   1 Timothy 2:1–3
4. John 16:22–26
5. Hebrews 4:13–16
6. Jude 20
7. Luke 18:1–14

Colossians 4:2

Prayer: Does It Work?
1. John 14:12–14
2. Acts 12:1–11

John 15:7

Fifteen Months of Nightly Readings

Scripture Reading	*Memory Verse*
3. Psalm 4:3	
4. Psalm 86:5–7	
5. Psalm 91:14–15	
6. Psalm 34:3–4	
7. Psalm 55:16–18	

1. Matthew 21:22	James 5:16b
2. John 15:5–7	
3. 1 John 5:14–15	
4. James 5:13–18	
5. Romans 8:15–16,26–27	
6. Colossians 2:1–2	
7. Daniel 6:3–10	

1. Mark 14:32–39	Psalm 4:4
2. Luke 5:15–16	
3. Joshua 10:13–14	
4. Mark 1:35 (Jesus prayed.)	
5. Mark 9:25–29	
6. 2 Corinthians 1:9–11	
7. Psalm 4:1–4	

What to Pray For:	Matthew 5:44
1. Matthew 5:44–48 Proverbs 29:10 (Pray for enemies.)	
2. Matthew 6:10–11 (Pray for God's will to be done; for daily food.)	
3. Matthew 6:12–13 (Pray for forgiveness, deliverance from evil.)	

Fifteen Months of Nightly Readings

Scripture Reading	*Memory Verse*

4. Luke 22:40
   Mark 14:38 (Pray that
   you enter not into
   temptation.)
5. Ezra 6:10
6. James 5:15–16 (Pray
   for the sick.)
7. Romans 10:1 (Pray
   for unbelievers.)

---

1. Ephesians 1:16–23   Ephesians 1:18–19
2. 2 Samuel 7:27
   Matthew 11:25
3. Jeremiah 33:3
   James 5:17–18
4. James 5:13
5. 1 John 5:16
6. Matthew 9:38
7. 2 Chronicles 7:14
   Ephesians 6:18–19

If You Feel Worried: Matthew 6:34
1. Proverbs 3:5–6
2. Psalm 55:17–19,22
3. Proverbs 20:24
   Psalm 124:8
4. Psalm 125:1–2
5. Matthew 6:25–34
6. Psalm 18:2–3
7. Psalm 18:30–36

Fifteen Months of Nightly Readings

Scripture Reading	*Memory Verse*
1. Isaiah 41:10–13	Isaiah 41:13
2. Luke 12:25	
3. Hebrews 13:6b,8	
4. Psalm 23	
5. Psalm 33:13–22	
6. Mark 4:35–41	
7. Psalm 121:1–8	

1. Philippians 4:6–7	Philippians 4:6–7
2. 1 John 4:16a,18	
3. Psalm 59:9,10a,16–17	
4. Psalm 27:1–6	
5. Psalm 27:14	
6. Psalm 56:3,8–12	
7. Luke 6:47–48	

1. Psalm 118:1,4,6	Psalm 118:6
2. Proverbs 19:23	
If You Feel All Alone:	
3. Psalm 54:4	
Psalm 14:5b	
4. Revelation 3:20	
5. Matthew 28:20b	
6. Joshua 1:9	
Ephesians 3:12	
7. 1 Peter 1:2	

1. Matthew 10:29–31	Matthew 10:29,31
2. Ephesians 2:9–13	
3. Ephesians 2:18–22	
4. 1 Peter 2:9b–10	
5. Romans 8:14–16	

Fifteen Months of Nightly Readings

Scripture Reading	Memory Verse
6. John 1:1–13	
7. John 14:15–19	

Scripture Reading	Memory Verse
1. John 16:27	Ephesians 3:17b–19a
2. Colossians 1:21–23	
3. Ephesians 3:17–21	
4. John 3:15–16	
5. 1 Corinthians 2:9	
6. Romans 8:35–39	
7. Romans 8:35–39 (repeat)	

Scripture Reading	Memory Verse
1. 1 Peter 5:7	1 Peter 5:7
2. Psalm 48:14	
Psalm 32:8	
3. 1 Chronicles 16:9	
4. Ephesians 1:4–5	
5. Hebrews 4:13	

God Protects You:
6. Proverbs 3:25
   Psalm 32:7
7. Psalm 9:1–11

Scripture Reading	Memory Verse
If You Feel Discouraged:	Isaiah 43:2a,3a
1. Psalm 42:1–11	
2. Psalm 130:1–7	
3. Psalm 31:2–12,19–21	
4. Jeremiah 20:11–18	
5. Psalm 102:1–7	
6. 1 Peter 5:7–11	
7. Psalm 43:1–3	
Ephesians 1:8	

Fifteen Months of Nightly Readings

Scripture Reading	*Memory Verse*
1. 2 Corinthians 1:3–5 Romans 8:28	Romans 8:28
2. Romans 15:13 1 Corinthians 2:9	
3. Psalm 147:5–6	
4. Philippians 4:4–7	
5. Psalm 34:17–19	
6. Exodus 2:23–25 Isaiah 49:13–15	
7. Psalm 40:1–4 John 14:18	

Is Jesus God?	John 1:1
1. Colossians 1:15–16	
2. Colossians 1:17	
3. John 1:1–3	
4. 1 Peter 2:22–25	
5. Mark 1:22	
6. 1 Timothy 3:16	
7. Matthew 3:13–17	

1. Matthew 17:1–8	Matthew 17:5b
2. Acts 3:11–15	
3. 1 Peter 1:18–21	
4. 1 Peter 3:22	
5. Matthew 16:15–16	
6. 2 Peter 1:16–18	
7. 1 Peter 1:19–20 Mark 15:33–39	

Fifteen Months of Nightly Readings

Scripture Reading	Memory Verse

1. Matthew 27:31,46–53   1 Peter 2:22–23
2. Matthew 14:23–33
3. John 1:10–12
4. John 1:18
5. John 1:32–36
6. John 3:33–36
7. John 20:20–29
   Luke 7:11–23

---

1. 1 John 5:6–10   John 14:6
2. John 3:9–18 (what Jesus
   said about Himself)
3. John 7:11–18
4. Matthew 26:63b–64
5. Matthew 27:11
6. John 8:12–16
7. John 8:53–58

---

1. John 14:6–11   John 8:12b
2. John 17:24–26
3. John 2:13–16
4. Matthew 11:27
5. Luke 10:21–22
   John 10:30–33
6. Matthew 28:20b
7. Mark 14:61–62
   Matthew 16:16–17
   (how Christ responded to
   Peter's calling Him God)

Fifteen Months of Nightly Readings

Scripture Reading	*Memory Verse*

Jesus Fulfilled Prophecy: — Micah 5:2
1. Micah 5:2–5
   Matthew 2:3–12
2. Isaiah 9:1–2
   John 8:12b
3. Isaiah 9:1–2 (repeat)
   Matthew 4:12–15
4. Matthew 12:14–21
5. Matthew 26:52–56
6. Acts 2:1–21
7. Isaiah 53:2–10 (repeat)
   1 Peter 2:21–25

---

1. Isaiah 7:14 — Isaiah 7:14
2. Matthew 1:18,22–23
   (fulfillment of
   Isaiah 7:14)
3. Micah 5:2
4. Luke 2:4,6–7 (fulfillment
   of Micah 5:2)
5. Psalm 16:10
   Acts 2:31–32 (fulfillment
   of Psalm 16:10)
6. Psalm 22:14–18,22
7. Matthew 27:35
   (fulfillment of Psalm 22)

---

1. Acts 2:22–32 — Acts 2:22
2. Psalm 22:18
3. Mark 15:22–24
   (fulfillment of above)

Fifteen Months of Nightly Readings

Scripture Reading	*Memory Verse*
4. Mark 14:21	
5. Romans 1:1–4	

Miracles Prove Jesus Is God:
6. Acts 2:22
7. Mark 16:20

1. Mark 5:1–20	Mark 6:56b
2. Mark 5:25–34	
3. Mark 5:35–43	
4. Mark 6:30–44	
5. Mark 6:46–56	
6. John 5:2–9a	
7. John 5:14–15,31–40	

1. John 10:22–42	John 10:30
2. Matthew 8:14–17	
3. Matthew 9:1–8	
4. Matthew 15:29–31 (Is Jesus God? He predicted His own death and resurrection.)	
5. Mark 10:32–34	
6. Matthew 16:15–20	
7. Matthew 16:21–23	

Jesus Rose from the Dead:	Romans 1:4a
1. Luke 18:31–33	
2. John 20:1–21	
3. Acts 3:15	
4. Romans 6:9–10	
5. Romans 1:4	

125

Fifteen Months of Nightly Readings

Scripture Reading	*Memory Verse*
6. 1 Corinthians 15:3–8	
7. 1 Corinthians 15:20	

1. Luke 24:36–43	1 Corinthians 3:16
2. Ephesians 1:19–20	
The Holy Spirit:	
3. 1 Corinthians 3:16	
4. Matthew 3:13–17	
5. Matthew 4:1–4	
6. Luke 11:13	
7. 2 Corinthians 3:18	

1. Romans 15:13	2 Corinthians 3:18
2. 1 John 2:27–29	
3. 2 Peter 1:20–21	
4. Ephesians 4:30–32	
5. John 14:15–27	
6. 1 Corinthians 2:7–16	
7. 1 Corinthians 12:1–7	

1. 2 Corinthians 1:21–22	Romans 8:11
2. Romans 8:4–10	
3. Romans 8:11–17	
4. Galatians 5:16–26	
5. Acts 9:31	
6. John 16:9–14	
7. Luke 2:25–31	

1. Luke 4:1–15	Ephesians 5:18b
2. Luke 4:16–21	
3. Luke 12:9–12	

Fifteen Months of Nightly Readings

Scripture Reading	Memory Verse
4. Ephesians 1:13–14	
5. Acts 2:1–18	
6. Ephesians 5:18	
7. Matthew 10:19–20	

1. Hebrews 3:6–11	Hebrews 3:6a
2. James 4:5–6	
3. Mark 13:11	
4. John 4:21–23	
5. 1 Corinthians 12:13	
6. 1 Thessalonians 1:5	
7. 1 Peter 1:2,10–12	

Jesus Is Coming Again: James 5:8b
1. Colossians 3:3–4
2. John 14:1–3
   James 5:7–9
3. 1 Peter 1:7
   Philippians 2:14–16
4. Acts 1:10–11
5. 1 Thessalonians 5:23
   1 Corinthians 1:7–9
6. 1 John 2:28
   Job 19:25
7. Daniel 7:1,9–14

1. Jeremiah 23:5–6	Mark 14:62
2. Psalm 50:1–6	
3. Zechariah 14:1–11	
4. Mark 14:61b–62	
5. Philippians 3:20	

Fifteen Months of Nightly Readings

Scripture Reading	Memory Verse

6. Review 1 Corinthians 1:7–9.
7. Review choice of verses above.

When Will the Second Coming Happen? — Luke 12:40
1. Matthew 24:14, 30–31,33,36–46
2. Luke 12:35–40
3. 1 Thessalonians 5:1–6 Matthew 24:27
4. 2 Thessalonians 2:1–12

Signs of His Coming:
5. Matthew 24:3–7
6. Daniel 12:4
7. Mark 13:10 Mark 10:32–37

---

1. 2 Peter 3:1–8 — 1 Thessalonians 4:17
2. Luke 17:26–37
3. 2 Timothy 3:1–8

How Will the Rapture Happen?
4. John 14:1–3
5. 1 Corinthians 15:51–58
6. 1 Thessalonians 4:15–18
7. Revelation 1:4–7

God Speaks to the Young: — Ecclesiastes 11:9
1. Ecclesiastes 11:9–10; 12:1–7,13

Fifteen Months of Nightly Readings

Scripture Reading	*Memory Verse*
2. 1 Timothy 4:12–16	
3. Matthew 18:5	
4. Psalm 34:11–17	
5. Jeremiah 1:4–8	
6. Proverbs 23:16–25	
7. Proverbs 23:31–35	

*Some Good Rules
to Live By:*   Proverbs 3:6
1. Proverbs 4:1–9
2. Proverbs 4:10–22
3. Proverbs 18:1–4
4. Proverbs 19:22–23
5. Proverbs 3:1–12
6. Matthew 26:41
7. Galatians 5:16–17

God Gives Instructions: 2 Timothy 3:16
1. 2 Timothy 3:16
2. 2 Timothy 4:1–4
3. Psalm 119:9–20
4. Proverbs 1:7–8
   2 Samuel 22:31
5. James 1:21–25
6. 1 John 2:27–28
7. John 14:15–17
   John 16:12–14

Knowing Right from Wrong: Psalm 25:4
1. James 1:5–8
2. Proverbs 2:1–10
3. Galatians 5:16,25

Fifteen Months of Nightly Readings

Scripture Reading	*Memory Verse*
4. Psalm 25:4–9 Proverbs 19:27 5. 1 Corinthians 6:11–13 6. Romans 14:23 7. Romans 15:1–3	
1. Mark 7:20–23 2. Proverbs 11:1–17 3. Deuteronomy 5:5b–21 4. Deuteronomy 6:1–9, 17–18 5. Isaiah 55:8–9 6. Proverbs 16:1–9,33 7. James 1:5	Deuteronomy 6:5–6
1. Matthew 7:7–11 2. Psalm 48:14 3. Psalm 73:23–24 4. Psalm 32:8 5. Psalm 18:33,36 6. Isaiah 58:11 7. Psalm 37:23–24	Psalm 18:33,36

1. Psalm 25:4–15
   Psalm 119:8
   Jeremiah 29:11–13
2. Micah 6:7–8
3. 1 John 4:7,21
*How Should Kids Treat
   Their Parents?*
4. Proverbs 6:20–23
	Micah 6:8

Fifteen Months of Nightly Readings

Scripture Reading	*Memory Verse*
5. Proverbs 15:5	
Proverbs 13:1	
Proverbs 19:26	
6. Proverbs 20:20	
Proverbs 23:22	
Proverbs 30:17	
7. Proverbs 28:24	
Proverbs 13:13	
Colossians 3:20	

1. Ephesians 6:1–3	Colossians 3:20
Exodus 21:15,17	
2. Deuteronomy 27:16	
3. Matthew 15:1–9	
4. Proverbs 30:1–14	
5. 1 Timothy 5:1–4	
6. Leviticus 20:6–9	
7. Colossians 3:20	

If You Have Done	1 John 1:9
Something Wrong:	
1. Ecclesiastes 7:20	
1 John 1:9	
Romans 3:23	
2. John 5:24	
3. Colossians 1:13–14,	
20–23	
4. Ephesians 1:4–7	
5. Psalm 103:1–12	
6. 1 Corinthians 1:8–9	
7. Colossians 2:13–15	

Fifteen Months of Nightly Readings

Scripture Reading	*Memory Verse*
1. 2 Corinthians 5:17–21	Acts 13:38b–39
2. Romans 8:29–34	

Forgiveness:
3. Romans 4:16–25
4. Acts 13:38–39
5. 1 John 1:8–10
6. Psalm 32:1–6

Jesus Forgave Others:
7. Luke 23:32–34

---

1. John 8:1–11   Psalm 86:5
2. Luke 15:11–24

*David's Prayers for
    Forgiveness:*
3. Psalm 86:5
    Psalm 130:1–5
4. Psalm 51:1–13
5. Romans 3:21–22
6. Psalm 34:17–19
7. Psalm 139:23–24

The Tongue: Matthew 12:35
1. Proverbs 10:14–19
    Proverbs 11:13
2. Proverbs 13:3
    Proverbs 15:26,28
3. Proverbs 18:6–8,21
4. Proverbs 26:20–22
5. Matthew 12:35–37
6. Matthew 15:16–20
7. Psalm 15:1–5

Fifteen Months of Nightly Readings

Scripture Reading	*Memory Verse*
1. Psalm 101:3–5	1 Peter 3:11
2. Psalm 141:2–4	
3. Jude 14–19	
4. 1 Peter 3:10–12	
5. James 3:1–12	
Isaiah 50:1–7	
(the way out)	

Overeating:
6. 1 Corinthians 6:12–13
7. Proverbs 13:25
   Proverbs 23:19–21

---

1. Proverbs 25:16	Philippians 2:13
2. 2 Peter 2:9	
(There is help.)	
Philippians 2:13	
3. Philippians 4:13	
(There is help.)	

Criticism and Correction:
4. Proverbs 10:17
   Proverbs 12:15
   Proverbs 13:18
5. Proverbs 15:31–32
   Proverbs 19:20
   Proverbs 23:12
6. Proverbs 25:11–12
   Proverbs 28:12–13
7. Proverbs 28:12–13
   (repeat)

How to Treat Our Bodies:	1 Corinthians 3:17
1. Romans 12:1	

Fifteen Months of Nightly Readings

Scripture Reading	*Memory Verse*

2. 1 Corinthians 6:19–20
3. 1 Peter 4:1–5
4. Proverbs 23:29–35
5. Proverbs 20:1
   Proverbs 31:4–6
6. Isaiah 5:11–25
7. 1 Samuel 30:16–20

---

1. 1 Timothy 5:22–23   Ephesians 4:32
2. Ephesians 5:18
   2 Peter 1:3–4

Arguing and Quarreling:
3. Philippians 2:14–15
4. 1 Timothy 4:7–8
5. Ephesians 4:31–32
6. James 1:19–20
7. James 4:1–3

---

1. Proverbs 11:12   Proverbs 15:1
   Proverbs 13:9–10
2. Proverbs 15:1
   Proverbs 18:1–3
   Proverbs 30:33
3. Proverbs 12:16–17
   Colossians 3:8
4. Proverbs 13:3
   Proverbs 14:17,29
5. Proverbs 16:24,32
   Proverbs 19:19
6. Proverbs 29:20–23
   Proverbs 22:24–25

Fifteen Months of Nightly Readings

Scripture Reading	*Memory Verse*

Swearing:
7. Exodus 20:7

---

1. Ephesians 5:3–4,6   Colossians 3:8,10
2. Matthew 12:33–37
3. Ephesians 4:29
   Luke 6:45
4. Proverbs 10:11
   Matthew 5:13,33–37
5. Colossians 3:8–10
6. Jude 24–25

Stealing:
7. Ephesians 4:28
   Isaiah 61:8

---

1. Proverbs 12:12   Psalm 32:6
   Proverbs 20:10
2. Psalm 101:1–4
   Psalm 32:1–9

Lying:
3. Ephesians 4:23–25
4. Psalm 6:12–19
5. Proverbs 12:13–14,19–20
6. Proverbs 13:5
   Proverbs 25:18
7. Proverbs 26:18–19

---

*What About Going   Exodus 20:11
to Church?*
1. Acts 2:41–47

Fifteen Months of Nightly Readings

Scripture Reading	Memory Verse

2. Luke 6:5–6
(Jesus attended
worship services.)
3. Hebrews 10:24–25
4. Acts 20:7
Acts 13:14
5. Exodus 20:8,11

Money:
6. Hebrews 10:34
7. Psalm 40:17
Proverbs 10:22
Psalm 102:17

---

1. Psalm 109:30–31	Matthew 6:34

    Psalm 69:29–33
2. Matthew 7:7–11
3. Matthew 6:25–34
4. 1 Corinthians 3:21–23
5. Proverbs 28:3
Philippians 3:7–9
6. Proverbs 15:6
Psalm 111:1–5
7. Psalm 37:16
James 2:5
James 1:9

---

1. Luke 6:17–25	Galatians 4:7

2. 1 Timothy 6:6–10
3. Proverbs 23:4–5
4. Psalm 112:1–3
5. Galatians 4:7

Fifteen Months of Nightly Readings

Scripture Reading	*Memory Verse*
6. Proverbs 8:1–11	
7. Proverbs 8:11–21	

1. Proverbs 27:24	Psalm 34:10b
Proverbs 11:24–28	
2. Matthew 6:31–33	
3. Psalm 34:9–11	
4. Ecclesiastes 5:10–12	
5. Isaiah 58:10–11	
6. Malachi 3:10	
Colossians 3:1–4	
7. Proverbs 3:13–18	

How Great God Is:	Jeremiah 32:27
1. Isaiah 40:12–27	
2. Proverbs 8:22–25	
3. Job 28:24–26	
4. Job 37:1–13	
5. Colossians 1:16–17	
6. Jeremiah 32:27	
7. Isaiah 48:12–13	
Isaiah 64:8	

1. 1 Chronicles 20:10b–13	Habakkuk 2:20
2. Colossians 2:3	
Romans 11:33–36	
3. Isaiah 43:10–13	
Isaiah 66:1–2	
4. Colossians 1:15–17	
5. Ephesians 3:20	
Isaiah 2:19–22	

Fifteen Months of Nightly Readings

Scripture Reading	Memory Verse
6. Jeremiah 16:20–21	
7. Jeremiah 17:9–10	
Habakkuk 2:20	

Scripture Reading	Memory Verse
1. 2 Chronicles 16:9	Acts 17:24
2. Psalm 107:23–43	
3. Acts 17:24–28	
4. Amos 4:13	
Amos 5:8–9	
5. Proverbs 30:4	
6. Psalm 104:1–17	
7. Psalm 104:18–35	

Scripture Reading	Memory Verse
1. Nahum 1:2–8	Psalm 90:2
2. Psalm 90:1–4	
3. Mark 4:35–41	
4. Habakkuk 3:3–6	
5. Psalm 139:15–18	
6. Isaiah 64:1–4	
7. Isaiah 40:10–26	

Scripture Reading	Memory Verse
How Much Does God Love Us?	John 3:16
1. John 3:16	
2. Romans 3:23	
3. Romans 8:35–39	
4. Ephesians 1:4–5	
5. Ephesians 3:17–19	
6. John 15:9–14	
7. 1 John 3:1	
1 Corinthians 2:9	

An Encouraging Word for Parents

Abraham Lincoln said, "A child is a person who is going to carry on what you have started. He is going to sit where you are sitting, and when you are gone, attend to those things which you think are important. You may adopt all the policies you please, but how they are carried out depends on him. He will assume control of your cities, states, and nations." Today's parents may need to decide soon if they want to maintain their right to raise tomorrow's leaders by the same biblical standards as our forefathers. Some are trying—and succeeding!

Last week I received a neat, hand-written letter on beautiful stationery from my bright and loving eleven-year-old granddaughter, Rachel. Rachel's parents have worked hard to pass the faith on to her and have somehow managed to spark her interest in the Bible. She also knows how to use her faith. After calmly telling me that she and her sister had successfully struggled through nasty bouts of malaria (no panic, just quiet and strong courage) and that she too wants to become a writer like me (smile), she closed on an upbeat note: "P.S. I finished reading the book of Leviticus. Mom said it would be boring, but I found it quite interesting. I'm sure glad I was taught how to study and appreciate the Bible."

I hope Rachel's terrific letter, showing her robust spiritual health, encourages parents that even in the unpredictable and sometimes scary nineties, children can hold fast to the satisfying comfort and stability that God offers to every generation. They do get interested in the Bible. Yours can too.

MORE HELPFUL RESOURCES FOR YOU AND YOUR CHILD

BIBLE REFERENCE TOOLS

Amplified Bible (Zondervan)

Bible Almanac: A Comprehensive Handbook of the People of the Bible and How They Lived, edited by James I. Packer, et al. (Thomas Nelson)

Bible Atlas, by Orrin Root (Standard)

Bible Dictionary for Young Readers, by William N. McElrath (Broadman)

Family Encyclopedia of the Bible (Chancellor)

Fun with Bible Geography, by Marie Chapman (Accent)

International Children's Bible Handbook, by Larry Richards (Word)

Nelson's Illustrated Bible Dictionary (Thomas Nelson)

The New Strong's Exhaustive Concordance of the Bible, in easy-to-read print with the words of Jesus highlighted (Thomas Nelson)

Pictorial Bible Dictionary (Zondervan)

ON THE BIBLE AND BASIC CHRISTIANITY

Bible Panorama, by Terry Hall (Victor)—shows how all the Bible facts fit together

Christian Theology in Plain Language, by Bruce Shelley (Word)

The Christian's Secret of a Happy Life, by Hannah W. Smith (Barbour and Co.)

The Dictionary of Biblical Literacy (Oliver Nelson)—a sweeping overview of biblical events, people, places, and concepts basic to understanding Christianity

The First Year of Your Christian Life, by Steven L. Pogue (Here's Life)

How We Got the Bible, by Neil R. Lightfoot (Baker)

Mere Christianity, by C. S. Lewis (MacMillan)

Milk for Babes, by Anne F. Murchison (Word)—questions that both unbelievers and new believers ask

More Than a Carpenter, by Josh McDowell (Tyndale)

Next Steps for New Christians, by Kenneth Taylor (Tyndale)

Talk Thru the Bible, by Bruce Wilkinson and Kenneth Boa (Thomas Nelson)—an upbeat survey of Bible books designed to give the big picture of biblical history

Thirty Days to Understanding Your Bible, by Max E. Anders (Wolgemuth & Hyatt)—a book that promises a good working knowledge of the history, chronology, and major doctrines of the Bible in fifteen minutes per day

What the Bible Is All About, by Henrietta C. Mears, et al., revised by Ronald Youngblood and Merrill C. Tenney (Regal)

What the Faith Is All About, by Elmer L. Towns (Tyndale)—a layman's approach to the Bible

Why I Believe, by James D. Kennedy (Word)

ON PRAYER

For Adults Only

Believer's Prayer Life, by Andrew Murray (Bethany House)

Conversing with God, by Rosalind Rinker (Zondervan)

How to Pray, by Reuben A. Torrey (Moody)

Love on Its Knees, by Dick Eastman (Revell)

Pray: God Is Listening, edited by Richard DeHaan (Zondervan)

The Prayer Factor, by Sammy Tippit (Moody)

Prayer: The Vital Link, by William J. Krutza (Judson)

Praying with the Bible, by Marilyn M. Helleberg (Abingdon)

Releasing God's Power, by Becky Tirabassi (Oliver Nelson)

What Happens When Women Pray, by Evelyn Christenson and Viola Blake (Victor)

When We Gather: A Book of Prayers for Worship, by James G. Kirk (Westminster John Knox)—a book of prayers for worship

For Children Only

I Can Pray to God, by Sandra Brooks (Standard)—a child's first book on prayer

I Can Talk to God Anytime, Anyplace, by Jennie Davis (Scripture)

Prayer Adventures for Boys and Girls, by Verna Nepstad (Sounds of His Coming, P.O. Box 8535, Fountain Valley, CA 92708)—a workbook to teach children how to pray and about the power of prayer

Prayer, How to Talk to God (BCM)

Prayers for the Young Child, by Don Roberts (Concordia)

Praying God's Way, by Richard Strout (Child Evangelism Fellowship)

ON INTRODUCING A CHILD TO CHRIST

Children and Conversion, by Clifford Ingle (Broadman)

Choosing to Be a Christian (Cokesbury)—a thirteen-session study designed to help fifth and sixth graders develop guidelines in decision making involved in becoming and being a Christian

God Wants You to Be a Member of His Family (Gospel Light)—a children's evangelism booklet

How to Become God's Child (Scripture Press)—a booklet to help a child understand what the gospel is all about

Jesus: God's Son, Savior, Lord, by Eugene Chamberlain (Broadman)

Tell All the Children, by Kenneth L. Chafin (Broadman)—how to witness to your child

What Can a Child Believe? by Eugene Chamberlain (Broadman)

RESOURCES FOR CREATIVE FAMILY WORSHIP

Acting Out the Gospels, by William DeAngelis (Twenty-third)—suggestions for using puppets, mimes, and clowns

Answers to Tough Questions Skeptics Ask about the Christian Faith, by Josh McDowell and Don Stewart (Campus Crusade)—the authors tackle sixty-five most-asked questions on the Bible, Jesus, miracles, creation, and other religions

Celebrations of the Heart and *Someone Cares,* by Helen Steiner Rice (Revell)—inspirational poems

Creative Family Times, by Hadidians and Wilsons (Moody)—activities to help young children develop character

Devotions for Families with Young Readers, by Barbara O. Webb (Judson)—thirty devotions that give young readers an opportunity to grow spiritually

Families Sharing God, by Barbara O. Webb (Judson)—thirty-five devotions for families

Family Night at Home, by Nancy Becker and Jack Braun, edited by Dennis Becker (Kindred)—helps in playing, sharing, and learning together as a family

Family Nights Throughout the Year, by Terry and Mimi Reilly (Abbey)—fifty-two year-round celebrations for families of all ages

Family Prayers, by John Wesley (Abingdon)

Family Worship Through the Year, by Kristen J. Ingram (Judson)—Christ-centered programs for daily devotions and special family occasions

Famous Prayers, by Veronica Zundel (Eerdmans)—a treasury of Christian prayers through the centuries

Finding God at Home: Family Life as a Spiritual Discipline, by Ernest Boyer, Jr. (Har-Row)

Good Clean Fun, by Tom Finley (Zondervan)—a collection of fifty nifty games, mazes, puzzles, brainteasers, and more, with built-in Bible lessons

Greatest Skits on Earth, by Wayne Rice and Mike Yaconelli (Zondervan)

Special Times with God and *More Special Times with God,* by David and Naomi Shibley (Thomas Nelson)

Worshiping with Your Child, by Richard S. Hanson (Abingdon)

Yearbook of Family Devotions (Children's Bible Hour, P.O. Box 1, Grand Rapids, MI 49501)—365 stories that apply the Bible to life today

Sources to Use with Young Children

Advanced Theology for Very Tiny Persons, by Doris Sanford (Multnomah)

Amazing Book—an animated video that teaches children about the Bible, for ages two through ten (Multnomah)

Bible in Pictures for Little Eyes, by Kenneth N. Taylor (Moody)—a book with cassette read by Chuck Wagner

Bible Lessons for Little People, by Evelyn Groggs and revised by Sarah Eberle (Standard)

Bible Rhymes to Say and Do, by Ruth Beechich (Accent)

Ethel Barrett Tells Favorite New Testament Stories—cassette tape (Regal)

Growing God's Way to See and Share, by V. Gilbert Beers (Victor)

Here a Little Child I Stand, edited by Cynthia Mitchell (Philomel)—poems of prayer and praise for children

International Children's Bible (Sweet)—award-winning low third-grade reading level to make Bible reading easier for children

Leading Little Ones to God: A Child's Book of Bible Teaching, by Marian M. Schoolland (Eerdmans)—a child's book of Bible doctrinal teachings

Little Visits with God, by Allan H. Jahsmann and Martin P. Simon (Concordia)—devotions for families with small children

Little Visits with Jesus, by Mary M. Simon (Concordia)

Love-A-Byes—sixty minutes of quiet songs of God's love on cassette tape to help lull little ones to sleep (Brentwood Music)

Mother Goose Gospel—children's favorite rhymes rewritten with a biblical twist, cassette with sing-along

Only for Children—animated cartoon videos that teach children moral integrity in solving problems (Word)

Read-N-Grow Picture Bible—features 1,870 colorful cartoon-strip illustrations that tell Bible stories

Stories for the Children's Hour, by Kenneth Taylor

(Moody)—insights into the behavior Jesus wants, with questions and answers after each chapter

Sources to Use with Juniors

Between You and Me, God, by Patricia A. Simmons (Broadman)—seventy-two prayers to help girls ages nine through twelve with problems of growing up

The Bible Tells Me So: God's Promises for Kids, by Merla Hammack and Lisa Williams

Cool: How a Kid Should Live, by Edythe Draper (Tyndale)—devotional readings for children ages eight through ten

Devotions for Junior High Girls, by Mary Lou Carney (Zondervan)

Family Time Bible Stories, by Anne deGraaf (Zondervan)—for reading aloud to all ages or for children ages ten through twelve to read on their own

Keys for Kids—a bi-monthly magazine with value-teaching stories to help kids cope with daily problems, for ages seven through fourteen; Children's Bible Hour, P.O. Box #1, Grand Rapids, MI 49501

Kids!—a magazine for nine- through thirteen-year-olds published nine times a year by Moody Bible Institute staff, 820 N. LaSalle Drive, Chicago, IL 60610, to help kids know God better with inspirational stories, games, jokes, sports articles

Pocketsful of Scripture, by Maryjane P. Norton (Upper Room)—shows kids how messages of the Bible fit into their daily lives

Pre-Teen Bible Studies for 8-12 Year Olds (Navpress)—combines stories, stickers, questions, and activities to help kids learn how to study the Bible on their own

Reading My Bible in Spring (Fall, Summer, Winter), by Lou Heath and Beth Taylor (Broadman)—daily devotions for children in grades one through six

Search—a Bible magazine for boys and girls, BCM International, 237 Fairfield Avenue, Upper Darby, PA 19082

Stretch, by Edythe Draper (Tyndale)—a daily devotional for children ages eleven through fourteen

Weathering Storms Books, by Sally Jordan and Diana Philbrook (Standard)—deal with issues faced by children in grades five through eight

What Does God Do? by Hans Wilhelm (Worthy)—God's answers to children taken from the International Children's Bible

What's the Good Word? the All New Incredible Bible Study Book for Junior Highs, by John C. Souter (Zondervan)

Sources to Use with Teens
Alive II, by S. Rickley Christian (Tyndale)—daily devotionals for youth

Alive Now—The Upper Room, 1908 Grand Avenue, Nashville, TN 37202; an inspirational contemporary magazine for older teens

Amazing Tension Getters, by David Lynn and Mike Yaconelli (Zondervan)—fifty-three real-life problems and predicaments, Scripture-based discussions

Big Questions, by Richard A. Kauffman (Herald)

Campus Journal—Radio Bible Class, Grand Rapids, MI 49555-0001; a monthly devotional booklet with teen topics

Campus Life—465 Gunderson Drive, Carol Stream, IL 60188; an upbeat monthly magazine for teens

Faces—an award-winning collection of prayers and poems for teens (Tyndale)

Good News Q's, by Fred Keiser (Zondervan)—questions to help high schoolers find answers, a devotional that guides through the gospels

Growing When You Don't Feel Like It, by Joyce M. Smith (Tyndale)—a Bible study for high schoolers

Hot Trax: Devotions for Guys and *Hot Trax: Devotions for Girls*, by Ken Abraham (Revell)

How to Keep Your Kids on Your Team, by Charles Stanley (Oliver Nelson)

How to Live with Your Parents Without Losing Your Mind, by Ken Davis (Zondervan)—tells teens how to make changes in their families by changing themselves, fun reading and fast moving

It's a Jungle in Here, by Dale and Sandy Larsen (Shaw)—realistic devotions for teens

Lifequest, by Jim Long (Tyndale)—personal stories and vivid writing to get kids excited about theology and doctrine

Mountain Trailways for Youth: Devotions for Young People, by Mrs. Charles E. Cowman (Zondervan)—a daily devotional for young people

Outtakes: Devotions for Girls/Guys, by Bill Sanders (Revell)

Pat Answers, by Pat Hurley (Word)—features 150 questions on the hottest and most troubling issues young people face

Preparing for Adolescence, by James Dobson (Bantam)—Dobson speaks directly to the adolescent about difficult issues in teen years; also on cassette

Take Five—Back to the Bible, P.O. Box 82808, Lincoln, NE 68501; a quarterly devotional magazine for teens

Teen Talks with God, by Robert Boden (Concordia)

Teenquest—Back to the Bible, P.O. Box 82808, Lincoln, NE 68501; monthly inspirational magazine for high school and early college age

Youthwalk—Walk Thru the Bible, P.O. Box 80587, Atlanta, GA 30366 or Focus on the Family,

Pomona, CA 91799; a topical daily devotions magazine for youth, published monthly, uses real life situations and Bible applications

BASIC RESOURCES ON PARENTING

For Two-Parent Families

Challenged Parenting, by Bonnie Wheeler (Regal)— suggestions for parents of handicapped children

Christian Home School, by Gregg Harris (Wolgemuth and Hyatt)

Don't Forget the Children, by Alan D. George (Radio Bible Class)

Forty Ways to Teach Your Child Values, by Paul Lewis (Tyndale)

God, Sex, and Your Child, by John Nieder (Thomas Nelson)

Heaven Help the Home!, by Howard G. Hendricks (Victor)

Helping Children Feel at Home in Church, by Margie Morris (Discipleship Resources)

Helping Your Child Discover Faith, by Delia T. Halverson (Judson)

How to Enjoy Raising Your Children, by Harold Sala (Accent)

How to Pray for Your Children journal, by Quin Sherrer (Servant)

How to Raise Christian Kids in a Non-Christian World, by Youth for Christ staff (Victor)

It's Never Too Early, by Grace Maberry and L. Barrett Smith (Discipleship Resources)—helping parents be religious with preschoolers

Nurturing Faith in the Family, by Jan and Myron Chartier (Judson)

Opening the Bible with Children: Beginning Bible Skills, by Patricia Griggs (Abingdon)

Raising Kids on Purpose, by Gwen Weising (Revell)

Sex Education Is for the Family, by Tim LaHaye (Zondervan)

Teaching Your Child About God, by Wes Haystead (Regal)

Together at Home, by Dean and Grace Merrill (Thomas Nelson)—helps parents explain Christian truths to grade schoolers

You and Your Child, by Charles R. Swindoll (Thomas Nelson)

Young Children and Worship, by Sonja M. Stewart and Jerome W. Berryman (Westminster John Knox)

For Single-Parent Families

Being Single Again, by J. Clark Hensley (Broadman)

Busy Person's Prayer Guide, by John C. Souter (Tyndale)

Christian Family Activities for One-Parent Families, by Bobbie Reed (Standard)—a year's activities for one-parent families

How to Single Parent, by Fitzhugh Dodson (Har-Row)

Just One of Me: Confessions of a Less-Than-Perfect Single Parent, by Dandi Daley Knorr (Shaw)

Know What You Believe, by Paul Little (Victor)—two easy-listening and time-saving cassettes about the basics of the faith

Single Mothers Raising Sons, Bobbie Reed (Thomas Nelson)

Single Parenting: A Wilderness Journey, by Robert G. Barnes, Jr. (Tyndale)

Single Parent's Survival Guide, by Robert G. Barnes, Jr. (Tyndale)

What's a Mother to Say?, by Ruth Vaughn (Warner)

When God Has Put You on Hold, by Bill Austin (Tyndale)

Other Ideas for Parents

Evangelizing Today's Child—2300 E. Highway M, Warrenton, MO 63383; a magazine published by Child Evangelism Fellowship to equip Christians to win children to Christ and disciple them

Lifewalk—Walk Thru the Bible, P.O. Box 80587, Atlanta, GA 30366; a contemporary topical daily

devotional monthly magazine geared to adults
with very little time

Teaching Aids for Parents of Mentally Impaired Children Are Available from:

David C. Cook Publishing, 850 N. Grove Avenue, Elgin, IL 60120

Broadman, 127 Ninth Avenue North, Nashville, TN 37234

BCM Publications, 237 Fairfield Avenue, Upper Darby, PA 19082

Scripture Press, 1825 College Avenue, Wheaton, IL 60187

About the Author

Alice Chapin loves children deeply and is a teacher, mother of four, and grandmother of ten. She has been on the staff of Campus Crusade for Christ, Military Ministry, along with her husband Norman, for the past eighteen years, teaching Bible studies and seminars on "How to Share Your Faith with Your Children" and other topics. Chapin is a member of the Authors' Guild and lives in Newnan, Georgia. She is also a member of the Chapel Community at Fort McPherson, Georgia.